ARMY OF THE CHURCH

By the same author

Evangelicals in Action (Bles)
Christians and Social Work (S.C.M. Press)

ARMY OF THE CHURCH

by

KATHLEEN HEASMAN, Ph.D.

Lecturer in Social Studies
Queen Elizabeth College, London

LONDON
LUTTERWORTH PRESS

267.16
H357

170793

7188 1340 5

Printed in Great Britain by
Latimer Trend & Co Ltd, Plymouth

Contents

Preface   *page* 7

THE FOUNDER AND HIS VISION   11

SPREADING THE GOSPEL   26
    In the Parish   30
    The Evangelistic Mission   35
    Touring the Countryside   38
    The Summer Crusades   42
    Children's Missions   44
    Training the Laity   47
    The Paraphernalia of Evangelism 51

THE SOCIAL WORK OF THE CHURCH ARMY   57
    The Homeless and Destitute   59
    Unattached Women and Girls   77
    Ordinary Families   92
    The Needs of the Younger Generation 102
    In and Out of Prison   111
    Somewhere to Live   122
    Retirement and its Problems 131
    Helping the Disabled   142

THE CALL OF OTHER COUNTRIES   146
    The United States and Canada 147
    Australia and New Zealand   152

India   *page* 156
East Africa   157
The Caribbean   161

THE CHURCH ARMY TODAY   165

Bibliography   175

Index   177

Preface

EVANGELISM HAS BEEN colourfully described as "one beggar telling another beggar how to find bread". This is what the Church Army has been doing since 1882. But its bread, like the manna in the wilderness, has been both spiritual and material nourishment. The Church Army has not only preached the Gospel; it has helped and cared for the needy. Both these tasks have fallen, with equal weight, upon its shoulders.

The Church Army is a society of the Church of England, and as such it abides by the discipline of that Church. Its ostensible purpose is to preach and teach the Word of God so that those who hear may be brought to a knowledge of Christ and eventually into the Church. But it also takes part in various forms of social work, and so can be regarded as a Church social work agency.

It is sometimes wondered how it manages to reconcile these two functions, for it is frequently thought that social work should be distinct from religious persuasion, and social workers should be people who are not apparently linked with any particular denomination. The answer lies in the work of Christ Himself who both taught and had compassion on those who came to Him for help. He understood to the uttermost the depths to which human nature could sink, and His deep seeking love was able to reach the personality which seemed beyond the range of any help.

The Church Army captains and sisters carry on their work in the belief that, through the grace of God, this is still possible. They find a spark of hope in every human

7

being, however degraded, and trust that by both offering
the material help that may be needed, and by presenting
Jesus Christ as a living person, the individual may be
helped to become more truly himself, and so better able to
cope with his circumstances. This mingling of social with
spiritual help is the contribution which a Church society,
like the Church Army, brings to the social work of this
country.

This book is not intended to supersede A. E. Reffold's
admirable book, *Wilson Carlile and the Church Army*, or indeed any of the accounts of its work which have been
written and are enumerated in the bibliography at the end
of this volume. It is an attempt to see the Church Army as
a group of people whose purpose is to demonstrate the
love of God both in what they say and in what they do. It
is an historical account of the linking together of evangelism and social work in such a way that help is offered to
the whole person, with the intention that he should be
enabled to become more truly himself.

The extensive quotations in this book are, unless otherwise stated, from the *Church Army Review*, which has been
published since 1894, and now is a bi-monthly magazine
describing the different aspects of Church Army work.
From its earliest numbers it has contained eye-witness
accounts, either from the pen of some Church Army
Officer or outside observer. Although, perhaps, such accounts are unduly glowing, there is little other material
available, except for the rather short annual reports, from
which most of the facts have been drawn. The only aspect
of the work of the Church Army which I have omitted is
their wartime work, and this can be found in J. K. V.
Durrell, *Whizz Bangs and Woodbines*, and D. H. Barber,
The Church Army in World War II.

So many people have helped me with information about
the Church Army that I hesitate to mention any personally, but I would like to thank all those captains and
sisters who have spared the time, in their busy lives, to

show me what they are doing and to tell me their remembrances of the past, among them Captain Amos Maina, in whose company I visited several of the lesser-known parts of Kenya where African Church Army officers are carrying on their work. I shall always remember with joy the very happy times I have spent with these captains and sisters, and their generous hospitality. Any opinions which are expressed, however, are not theirs, nor those of the Church Army, but my own. Miss Vera Bowen has typed my manuscript, and, as always, I am very grateful to her for her care and forbearance. Once again, my husband has proved indefatigable in reading the manuscript, and in encouraging me when enthusiasm has flagged. And I should like to mention the Reverend Donald Knight who, when vicar of St. Paul's, Beckenham, first introduced me to the work of the Church Army.

Queen Elizabeth College   K.J.H.
London University
December, 1967

CHAPTER I

The Founder and His Vision

ONE RARELY visits the home or office of a Church Army officer without finding a photograph of "The Chief" in some prominent place. Wilson Carlile has inspired generations of captains and sisters with his infectious desire to help other people, whatever their needs, and so to bring them closer to God.

Conversion, consecration and churchmanship were his three basic objectives—the three C's, as he would jocularly call them. First, he was determined to help people to respond to the love of God, and there were no limits to the methods which he was willing to adopt in order to achieve this. Then he was concerned with teaching people how to abide in God's love, and much of the work of the Church Army has been to help Christians in their daily lives. Finally, he was intent upon encouraging people to become loyal members of a Christian community, and, since the Church Army was a Church society, this meant the Anglican Church.

This had not always been the purpose of Wilson Carlile. At the beginning of the 1870's he was a typical young businessman. He came from a successful, middle-class family; he had the gifts of physical health and strength which enabled him to cover the five and a half miles to his office each morning on foot; he was ambitious and his colleagues expected him to do well in the business world. In fact, he had determined to make £20,000 before his twenty-fifth birthday, and when that birthday came he had made well over this amount.

England was, at that time, at the height of her prosperity and power. Her trade was extensive and her industrial life thriving. Profits were rising, large fortunes were being made, and there was a general air of success and well-being, especially among the middle class. Then, in 1873, the great depression started, and lasted with only short breaks until 1896. Like any business depression of that time, it caused poverty, unemployment and distress to the working people, but it was a depression of prices and profits in the first instance, and so it had immediate and disastrous effects upon many business men.

Wilson Carlile was among those successful businessmen who were severely hit by the events of 1873. On the so-called "Black Friday" the business in the City of London which he had taken over from his grandfather failed, and the prosperity which he had built up was brought to a sudden end. Mental strain led to a physical breakdown, and for many weeks he was forced to lie idle in bed. All his energies until now had been engaged in acquiring material wealth and position, and seemingly with little use. What, then, was the purpose of life?

Like so many people, he sifted over in his mind the various answers which others had given to this question, but without any satisfaction, until he happened to read Mackay's *Grace and Truth*. Then, in a flash, he found what he had been looking for. He used to say in later years: "I have seen the crucified and risen Lord as truly as if He had made Himself visible to my bodily sight. That is for me the conclusive evidence of His existence. He touched my heart, and old desires and hopes left it. In their place came the new thought that I might serve Him and His poor and suffering brethren." He was one of those fortunate people who, once having grasped the Christian faith, had no doubts at all as to its meaning, and his new-found singleness of mind gave him the drive which was to lead him through the many difficulties and seemingly impossible situations of the future.

The eldest of a family of twelve, Wilson Carlile had been born in 1847, and had spent his early years in Brixton. As a child he was not particularly outstanding, but always concentrated on anything which interested him. Music was his great delight, and before he was three his mother had found him standing on tiptoe in front of the piano with his hands outstretched above his head, striking some notes. The chords which he played pleased him, and he asked her to help him play others. From then onward, much of his spare time was spent on music.

Like many musical people, he was also good at languages; when at the age of fourteen he was sent to school in France for a short time, he quickly learnt to speak French, and in later life became proficient in both German and Italian. But business was to be his career, and on his return from France he joined his grandfather's firm and, at the age of eighteen, on account of his grandfather's health, found himself more or less in control.

He had set his heart on being a success, and so the failure of this business in 1873 destroyed all his dreams. After he recovered from his breakdown his father took him into his own business, and he worked for several more years in the City, but his real interest now lay in religious work. This was the time when Dwight L. Moody, the famous American evangelist, made his second and most successful visit to this country and held his great rallies in the Agricultural Hall, Islington. Wilson Carlile offered his help in the only way he knew, and that was with the music. Ira Sankey, the musical director, soon realized his ability, and placed him at the harmonium where he accompanied the singing of the vast crowds which came to hear Moody. He attended the whole of the mission at the Agricultural Hall, and then went with Moody to Camberwell, where he selected and trained the choir for the South London mission. Thus he gained, at first hand, an intimate knowledge of the techniques of evangelism and the part which music could play, and this knowledge was to stand him in good stead when he became the leader of the Church Army.

But Moody taught him more than this. He learnt the essentials of his new-found faith, and he became inspired with the ambition of becoming an evangelist. The Evangelization Society had been training laymen, since 1864, in the art of evangelism, and had been sending them to preach in churches, schools, missions, and the open air. Wilson Carlile, therefore, offered his services. But his preaching was not entirely acceptable to the Society, and he only stayed with them for a short time. He did, however, learn much about the methods and value of lay preaching, and the need for the layman in all types of evangelism.

At this time his thoughts were turning towards the ministry of the Church of England. He had not always been an Anglican. In his youth he had gone to the Congregational Church at Stockwell, and for a time after his conversion he had been a member of the Plymouth Brethren. But his father's connexion with Holy Trinity, Richmond, encouraged him to join the Anglican communion, and this was a step which was to influence his whole future. He had learnt from the Brethren the value of the breaking of bread every Sunday morning, and he found in the Church of England the order and the discipline which he craved, and which were to play an important role in the methods of the Church Army.

His decision to take Holy Orders was followed by his acceptance as a student at the London College of Divinity, which was then at Highbury, and after eighteen months he had passed his examinations, been ordained a deacon in St. Paul's Cathedral in Lent 1880, and accepted as a curate by Dr. Carr-Glyn at St. Mary Abbots, Kensington.

This was an ideal church in which to serve his apprenticeship, for he was one among several curates of all degrees of churchmanship, and this helped him to realize the contribution which each could make to the Church as a whole. His vicar was a man of deep understanding and, though he might not agree with the unconventional methods which Wilson Carlile used, he gave him the support he needed, and, when these methods proved unacceptable in this highly respectable parish, he encouraged him to use them elsewhere. Thus, unlike some similar movements which were lost to the Church, the Church Army became firmly entrenched within the bounds of the Church of England.

Wilson Carlile had applied for this curacy principally because it involved the care of the soldiers who constituted the guard at Kensington Palace, and he hoped through them to reach people who were unfamiliar with, or unacceptable at the churches. Charles Booth, writing at that time said: "The churches have come to be regarded as the resorts of the well-to-do, and of those who are willing to accept the charity and patronage of people better off than themselves." Few of the ordinary working people in the towns ever darkened the doors of their parish church, and in most cases would have found no welcome had they done so. Wilson Carlile was determined that this should not be the case of any church where he ministered. He would bring Christianity to the people in a way which was comprehensible to them, and break down this barrier between those within the churches and those outside.

This was by no means easy in the daughter church of St. Paul, Kensington, of which he was the priest-in-charge, for the poorer people would not come to the ordinary services, and if they had come, his congregation would have left him. Therefore he started late Sunday evening meetings in the church school, using some of the evangelistic methods with which he was familiar. But in spite of the magic lantern and well-known hymns accompanied by wind and other instruments, the attendances were small and did not attract the people whom he wished to reach. So he decided to hold open-air meetings on the small piece of ground between Kensington High Street

and St. Mary Abbots, where the old police station now
stands, in order to attract the many people as they passed
down the street.

> If you had been there, what would you have seen? A hand-
> some, virile young man with a complete disregard for cus-
> tom and convention, joyously alive and eagerly anxious to
> get his message across, his face lit up by humour and love.
> Even in a crowd, he made each man feel he was specially
> addressing him.

Soon he needed others to help him, and these he drew
from those who had attended the indoor meetings. At first
they were shy, and few were accomplished speakers, but
their simple testimonies to their faith appealed to the
crowds. People gathered in large numbers, and the police
were obliged to move them on. Complaints were lodged,
and Dr. Carr-Glyn had to tell his unusual curate that such
meetings must stop. Nevertheless, he urged him to continue them elsewhere; and so, with his vicar's consent,
Wilson Carlile resigned his curacy to devote his time to
slum missions.

Slum missions were a characteristic of Victorian
England, and most of them, like St. Giles Christian Mission and the Tower Hamlets Mission, preached to the
people and also provided them with much needed social
services. But most of them were middle-class interdeno-
minational ventures. Wilson Carlile wanted to use the
working man to help his fellow workers, and to do so
within the structure of the Church of England.

He may first have gained the idea from the Rev. Evan
Hopkins, the vicar of the church where he had worshipped
in Richmond, who had started a Church Gospel Army to
evangelize his parish. Canon Atherton was doing similar
work at Bristol, and other vicars were beginning to use
laymen as full-time evangelists in their parishes.

Wilson Carlile felt that if small efforts like these could be
co-ordinated, then trained evangelists could be sent to any
parishes whenever they were required. It was a somewhat

pretentious idea, and Wilson Carlile had to start in a small way, under the auspices of the Church Parochial Mission Society, but within a short time he was able to sever this connexion and to forge ahead on his own. Thus, in 1882, the Church Army was born.

Wilson Carlile was often asked in later years why he called his society an "army", and he usually replied, because his evangelists were intended to make war against sin and the devil. The years in which the Church Army grew up were militant ones. The Franco-German war had preceded the formation of the Church Army by a little more than a decade, and Wilson Carlile had visited France at the time and seen much of the devastation which had been caused. The Boer War was to take place less than twenty years after its formation, and people were very conscious of the need for adequate armed forces. Reforms had been undertaken within the army itself; short service commissions introduced, and an army reserve formed. Thus the people were "army conscious", and well understood what the term "army" was meant to convey. They were quite willing to accept the significance of army ranks, and in fact many societies, like the Salvation Army and the Boys' Brigade, were organized in this way.

An essential part of an army is its discipline, and, from the first, Church Army officers were expected to obey implicitly the orders of the Chief. Wilson Carlile was a masterful man. He disliked committees, and chafed against advice; and was always oppressed by the conventions and deadening routine which often marks the normal life of a church. Therefore, it is not without significance that there was one supreme leader and one supreme will. His comrades rarely resented his masterful ways, because they were inspired by his personality and the rightness of his cause. But, as in the case of the Salvation Army, this did sometimes cause difficulties, especially later on, when, in a more democratic age, it was impossible to exercise the same degree of undivided authority.

B

But the Church Army has never made any pretensions to be anything but a society within the Church of England. Wilson Carlile was always a man under authority in this respect. Episcopal sanction and benediction were always obtained before any work was undertaken in a diocese. No religious work was carried out in any parish without the approval of the incumbent, nor in any prison or public institution unless invited by the chaplain. Similarly, the permission of the Convocations had to be sought when Church Army evangelists and sisters were admitted to definite offices within the Church.

The first Church Army press notice appears in 1882, and reads:

> The "Church Army" has commenced at Walworth. Its nightly procession, consisting of a clergyman with a banner, half a dozen lady workers and a number of laity, has been pelted with cabbage stumps and rotten apples.

The Walworth mission was followed by one of a more permanent nature with its centre at the Portcullis Hall, Westminster. This excited intense hostility on the part of some of the inhabitants, particularly a group known as the "skeleton army", a collection of toughs who had as their object the breaking up of outdoor religious meetings and processions. Day after day the Church Army was assailed with missiles and all forms of violence. Wilson Carlile refused to prosecute, and he had his reward in winning some of his worst assailants. But this exasperated the mob to such an extent that eventually a savage and brutal attack was made upon Wilson Carlile himself, who was knocked down, trampled on, and narrowly escaped with his life. But, like most forms of persecution, this helped rather than hindered the work.

This mission was only a beginning. Wilson Carlile's purpose was to establish similar work throughout the parishes of England. Therefore, as soon as he could leave the Westminster mission in safe hands he devoted his time to publicity. He received short shrift from the Church Congress in

1883 where he had gone to plead for a chance to be given to trained lay people to help in evangelistic work within the Church. But there were some clergy and laity who welcomed the idea, and in order to arrest their sympathy and support Wilson Carlile started, in 1884, upon a personal campaign, visiting the principal provincial cities and addressing clerical and public meetings about the Church Army's aims, ideas and methods.

This led, in February 1885, to the Upper House of the Convocation of Canterbury unanimously passing a resolution of approval. In the same year the Bishop of Newcastle widely praised the work of the Church Army at the Portsmouth Church Congress, and Wilson Carlile, who was one of the invited speakers, was heard this time patiently, though not with enthusiasm. Two years later, the Church Army was, for the first time, recommended in a bishop's charge to his parishes as being able to "effect what no existing parochial organization could have effected".

Thus the Church Army gradually gained the respect, and often the love, of the Church, largely because it has never been hampered by party ties. It has maintained an independent position, friendly with all parties in the Church, but bound to the allegiance of none.

The Church Army was now gradually growing in strength. At the first annual conference of officers and workers in January 1885 Wilson Carlile reported:

> A year ago we had fifteen working-men evangelists, in addition to our honorary staff. Now we have forty-five wholly engaged in the work, while many parishes maintain a Church Army corps with the aid of local officers. We have between four and five thousand active members—many of them at one time drunkards, gamblers, wife-beaters, blasphemers, and others—who are now workers in the cause of Christ. Our income for the past year was £2,500 in regular subscriptions, besides over £4,000 in working people's pence.

The next year the annual report stated that

sixty-five evangelists were then giving their whole time to the work, assisted by six thousand communicant members, who were voluntary helpers; twenty thousand open-air and twenty thousand indoor meetings had been held in the year, attended by three million people.

Social work was soon forced upon the Church Army, for England in the 1880's was a very different place from what it is today. Wages were low, work intermittent and poverty imminent for those who at the best of times could only just manage to exist upon the income which they earned. This was made worse by the high rents charged in the towns. Few families could afford more than one room, many had to share, and some could pay no rent at all. The Royal Commission on the Housing of the Working Classes in 1885 found that large numbers of houses "have no wash-houses, no backyard, no back ventilation, and the owners are as a rule non-residential. The street doors are rarely shut so that staircases and passages at night are always liable to be crowded by persons who come to sleep. The custom is so casual in the worst parts of London, that in the Mint, Southwark, some people are known as 'appy dossers' ". It was such people as these "appy dossers" who attended the Church Army meetings, and it became quite obvious that if Christianity was to be commended to them, it would have to be accompanied by some forms of material help as well.

So the Church Army began to help those who were genuinely in need. As the annual report of 1902 puts it:

> The work of the Church Army is divided into Evangelistic and Social departments, but every year the Evangelistic department becomes more Social and the Social more Evangelistic.

Wilson Carlile, writing in 1922, says:

> In the Church Army we believe that "Inasmuch as ye have done it unto one of the least of these my brethren, ye have done it unto Me". We see the opportunity of ministering to Christ in ministering to the man in the prison cell, to the

prisoner's wife starving at home, to the lonely dying man, to the "down-and-out" tempted to suicide, to the orphan child. Here, as in the purely evangelistic work, we minister to the individual soul through the body.

Christians have often found it difficult to decide the relative importance of preaching the Gospel and helping other people. This was a problem which tried the minds of many in the late nineteenth century. The Church Army has always managed to combine the two, for they found in the early days that when a person was in need he would rarely respond to preaching, but if help was given to him, and this help was the expression of a loving concern, then the result was likely to be different. It was upon this basis that the social work of the Church Army was gradually built up. As times have changed, so have the forms of Church Army social work, but the basic motive has always been the same.

This growing task of evangelism and social work required careful organization, and Wilson Carlile was well equipped for this by his early business training.

At first the Church Army was administered from the offices of the Church Parochial Mission Society, but when this connexion was severed, it was necessary to find somewhere as headquarters for the new society and as a training home for its recruits. Marble Arch seemed a suitable area. Hyde Park was close by, where open-air meetings could be held, and the streets round the Edgware Road were places where poor and undesirable characters tended to congregate. 128 and 130 Edgware Road fell vacant and were purchased in 1886 on a thirty-eight years' lease, and they formed the first headquarters of the Society and the training home until 1903.

The greater part of a block between Cumberland Mews and Bryanston Street was then acquired, and on it was built a five-storied building which comprised the central headquarters and the new training homes for men and for women; and when the remainder of the block was purchased in 1908, a large conference hall, refreshment and recreation rooms were added. This island site near Marble Arch remained the headquarters of the Society until 1964, when its familiar surroundings were exchanged for the present multi-storied building on the site of the old Yorkshire Stingo Brewery in the Marylebone Road.

In spite of the administrative work involved, Wilson Carlile continued to fulfil his duties as a parish priest, and from 1892 to 1926 he was rector of St. Mary-at-Hill, Eastcheap. The living was originally given to him to provide him with some income, for he never drew any salary for his work with the Church Army. Yet, although there were few residents who dwelt in this City parish, he did not let his job remain a sinecure. People from far and near would come on Sundays to the nine o'clock Communion service followed by breakfast, and then, led by their rector, they would march to Petticoat Lane or Spitalfields for an open-air service. In the evening, he would collect his congregation by marching through Eastcheap and King William Street to London Bridge and back again, and there would follow the usual evening service, with the prayers and hymns thrown on to a screen so that those not familiar with the Prayer Book could take part. Objections were sometimes raised to the sensational titles which he used for his sermons, yet it was these which drew so many and varied people, and which probably accounted for the large proportion of men in his congregation.

Wilson Carlile could never have achieved all this without the unwavering support of his family and friends. Mrs. Carlile, though at first somewhat daunted at the change in her husband's plans, for they had been married in 1870 when he was still successfully engaged in business, was always in sympathy with him. She must have had many anxious moments, for in his work in Kensington, and later at Westminster, he was frequently in danger from the ruffians who tried to break up the meetings. It is said that after these meetings a worker was asked to knock three times on the door of the Carliles' house on her way home, so that Mrs. Carlile might know that all was well. After her death in 1925, Wilson Carlile lived with his sisters in their home at Woking.

One of his sisters, Marie Carlile, had from the first taken great interest in his work. In 1888 she volunteered to help her brother, and, although it was her intention to stay for only a few weeks, this proved the beginning of a service for the Church Army which lasted well over fifty years. She undertook the training of the sisters, and managed the women's work. What Wilson Carlile was to the men, Marie Carlile was to the women. Her counsel, her modifying influence, her alert instinct, and her ready humour often helped to ease a difficult situation, and to bring about a balanced judgement when tempers were frayed.

Several other ladies were closely associated with the Society in its early days, among them Miss Gay and Miss Cheshire. Evelyn Gay was a close friend of the family, especially of Marie Carlile and of her youngest sister, Janet. From her vast experience of social work among girls in the East End of London, she was able to advise Marie Carlile upon the special circumstances of many women who came to the Church Army for help. Mary Cheshire was the chief publicity agent of the Church Army for many years, helping to edit the first issues of the *Battleaxe*, which preceded the *Church Army Gazette*. As one of the first lady supporters, she had taken her share of the red ochre, flour, beer and rotten eggs thrown during the scuffles in Westminster.

Perhaps the person nearest to Wilson Carlile in these early days was Edward Clifford. They had probably first met at the Moody meetings in the Agricultural Hall, in 1875, and, as members of the sub-committee of the Church Parochial Mission Society which directed the formation of the Church Army, they came closely into contact. The first captain to be commissioned writes of him:

he would often carry and beat the drum, the only instrument we had. He often saved it from the knives on entering the room by holding it above the heads of the roughs. On one occasion he was beating the drum, and he was going up a narrow court, and he got the drum wedged; we had it rather warm with the roughs behind us, but nobody killed. The work went on, and he stuck to it like a hero.

Though his real interest was in art and travelling, he became, in the less turbulent days, the evangelistic secretary, and was responsible for the training of the early officers. He would write them letters of encouragement and advice, which can still be read in *The Blue Distance* and *A Green Pasture*. If their Victorian modes of expression are overlooked they could well have been written today. When he died in 1907 he was greatly missed.

Wilson Carlile gathered round him a number of other friends, some of whom were voluntary workers, others commissioned Church Army officers; and it was their staunch support and advice which made possible the growth and development of the Church Army. Though he might have been forbidding to those who opposed him, he was essentially a friendly man, and had a knowledge of and took an interest in the affairs of everyone with whom he worked. Right up to his death in 1942 he was lovingly known as The Chief, and is still remembered as such. He welded the members of the Church Army into a family, and it is largely due to his concern for each one that this spirit has been fostered and maintained. This intimate relationship between the head and the members has continued with each of the subsequent "chiefs"—Prebendary Treacher, who managed the affairs of the Church Army until ill-health forced him to resign in 1949; the Rev. Edward Wilson Carlile, the grandson of the founder, who succeeded Prebendary Treacher and was chief secretary until 1960; and Prebendary Donald Lynch, the present chief secretary.

The secret of his vision was revealed by Dr. W. R.

Matthews, then Dean of St. Paul's, in words spoken at the first Founder's Day Service in January 1943:

The keynote of his life was a profound belief and experience in the reality of conversion; and in this he was only carrying on the distinctive note of Christianity, that which differentiates it from all other doctrines of God, namely, that God is not only the God who is willing to forgive, but He is the God who goes out to seek and to save those who are lost. It was this profound conviction which was the mainspring of everything that he did. The social work was a notable achievement; but its foundation, its main thing in the Chief's eye, was the salvation of the individual soul. And is not that needed today as much as ever, perhaps more than ever? Wilson Carlile would bear his testimony that the main concern of the Church and of Christians is not to produce blue prints of a secular Utopia, but to proclaim the love of God to the individual and to believe, what is surely very evident, that the good society will only grow out of the good soul, and that the good soul is one which is surrendered to Christ and lives in His Spirit.

CHAPTER II

Spreading the Gospel

THE PRIMARY AIM of every captain and sister is to help
those who come their way to understand the full meaning
of Christianity. Thus, candidates for the Church Army,
when they have successfully finished their training are
first admitted to the office of evangelist in the Church of
England, and are then commissioned as captains and
sisters of the Church Army. At the first of these services,
like the early apostles, they are commanded "to go forth
into the world in peace; be of good courage; hold fast
that which is good; render to no man evil for evil;
strengthen the fainthearted; support the weak; help the
afflicted; honour all men; love and serve the Lord, re-
joicing in the power of the Holy Spirit". At the second
service they are received into the family of the Church
Army, and given into the care of the department with
which they are to serve.

The first Church Army evangelists were the men and
women in the Kensington parish of St. Mary Abbots
who helped Wilson Carlile by giving out a hymn or by
explaining a verse of scripture which had appealed to
them. It was then felt that something more formal was
required, and so members were enrolled. In 1883 an
enrolled member of the Church Army had to have been a
probationer for at least one month, and promise obedience
to the rules and regulations, which included "a spirit of
cheerful endurance under trial or difficulty, a spirit of
patient forbearance towards all who oppose, and a spirit

of loving submission one to another". It soon became apparent that some sort of training must be given, and so the Church Army committee started a training home at Oxford, where the Rev. F. S. Webster, who had been a friend of Wilson Carlile in Richmond, was the first principal. As Oxford was too far away, it was decided in 1885 to move to London, and rooms were taken over a jeweller's shop at 174 Edgware Road. Though changing its location several times, the men's training home remained in this area until after the second world war, and for much of the time was in the block of buildings which housed the headquarters.

This locality was particularly suitable, for it was close to Hyde Park, where much of the training in public speaking took place. The usual programme for a Sunday evening was prayer and preparation at 4.30 p.m., an open air meeting in the Park at 5 p.m. where both experienced and inexperienced were liable to be called upon to speak, and "fishing" from 6 p.m. to 6.30 p.m. which meant inviting passers-by to come to an evangelistic service in the Brunswick Chapel. This connexion with the Brunswick Chapel, Upper Berkeley Street, dates back to the very early days, when the first principal of the men's training home arranged for it to be their regular place of worship. Through the generosity of Lord Portman it became the headquarters church of the Society, and a mission centre for much of the work of the training homes. Now, with the beautiful chapel in the new headquarters, and the moving of the training college to the suburbs, it is no longer needed, and so has been given up.

The Church Army "nurses", as the commissioned sisters of the Church Army were called in the early days, had their first training home in Little Queen Street, just off the Edgware Road. Several subsequent moves were made in the district, and during the last war, when the home had to be evacuated, they took over The Waldrons, at Croydon as a temporary home. Men's and women's training at this time were entirely separate, though they did sometimes attend the same lectures, but after the last war it was felt that much of their training could be united, so, when a large country house at Maiden Erleigh, near Reading, was used for the purpose, both men and women were housed together.

It was hoped to use the money which had been collected as a memorial to Wilson Carlile for a new training home to be built, when hostilities ceased, on a site in Roehampton. But this site was requisitioned for other purposes, and as Maiden Erleigh was rather far from headquarters, it was decided to move back to London, and use the Church Army premises in Cosway Street, Marylebone, as a temporary measure until a new training college could be built. St. Christopher's, a Church training college at Blackheath, was eventually acquired in 1964, and adapted for the purpose by the building of a chapel and a wing of study-bedrooms for the brothers and sisters in training.

The types of people who offer themselves for training have not varied greatly throughout the years. They have nearly always given up some more lucrative employment, and they sometimes bring with them skills like carpentry or nursing which can be put to good use. But, whereas in the past it was usually people from the lower income groups who applied, now trainees come from all social groups, and even from overseas and as far afield as the Caribbean and East Africa.

In 1890 the training consisted of lectures and instruction in the Bible and the Prayer Book, in the playing of such instruments as the cornet, the concertina and the harmonium, in singing, in ambulance classes, and in methods of visiting and of conducting open-air and evangelistic meetings. It was quite short, for the captains and sisters were urgently required in the field. By the 1950's they were taking the London University Certificate of Proficiency in Religious Knowledge, and the Theology and Pastoral Examination of the Central Council for Women's

Church Work. A variety of outside activities, such as meetings in Hyde Park and the Edgware Road, guides and scouts, Sunday school teaching and youth club work, have always formed part of the training, and the students spend their vacations gaining experience in different forms of Church Army work.

Until 1937 the training lasted for one year. Then it was increased to two years and now costs several hundred pounds per student. Local authority grants and Church Army bursaries are available, so that no one is prevented by financial reasons from taking the training.

A wider training in social work, and an understanding of some of the basic principles of psychology are some of the things required today, and they are gradually being introduced into the course.

Work is provided by the Church Army for all who are commissioned, and most stay with the Society throughout their lives, though some move on to other forms of Christian work, and a number of the captains have been ordained as clergymen. In recent years there has been a shortage of suitable candidates, especially women, and therefore in 1960 a shortened course was introduced for women between thirty-five and fifty to work in the social departments. Their training was practical rather than theoretical and they spent much of it in the field. It was hoped to attract the more mature person who for one reason or another had been unable to apply at an earlier age.

But the basic part of the training is the development of personality. Captains and sisters have to be able to talk readily and easily to all sorts of people, and to make them feel that they are there to listen to other people's troubles. For it is only when a person is entirely at ease that he is likely to be responsive to the word of God. Life at the training college tries to teach this, with its discipline, its mingling of types of people, and its essentially communal form of life. All who go to the college learn something of the joy of living with others, but they also learn the value of solitude, for the chapel is always open for prayer, and the single study-bedrooms make quiet reading and meditation possible.

When the brothers and sisters in training are commissioned, they are called upon to do various types of work, and may pass from one department to another. Many choose to concentrate on evangelism, and this, too, can take a variety of forms. They may be evangelists on the staff of a parish. They may be involved in some special effort to reach people through a local mission or on one of the vans which travels over the countryside. They may take part in a summer crusade or a seaside mission. They may be seconded to work with the children's missions. In each of these ways they will be fulfilling their promise as an evangelist to take the word of God to the people.

<h2 style="text-align:center">IN THE PARISH</h2>

As would be expected, much of their work takes place within a parish, and throughout the years the majority of those commissioned have been placed in the men's or women's parochial departments. A captain, speaking at a recent conference of the men's parochial department, said:

> I remind myself that our beloved Society was born in a parish and that the old Chief, far from feeling "cabin'd, cribbed, confin'd", found his true outlet in the parochial set-up.

Parochial work is the backbone of the rest of the work of the Church Army, and yet it is probably an aspect of the work which is the least known.

The parochial captain or sister is always invited by the incumbent of the parish to work on his staff, and the fact that he or she holds the office of an evangelist provides a distinctive ministry from that of the incumbent who generally has to put his pastoral work first. Though a captain or sister usually takes part in the everyday life of the parish, an important part of the work is directed toward those who do not attend church. Parishes differ widely, and so in each case the ways of reaching such people have to be thought out afresh, and each Church Army officer is constantly changing and adapting his or her methods to meet the needs of the people.

A day in the life of a parochial evangelist in 1902 started with

> morning prayer in the Church, then back home to prepare his address for the evening. Next came time for visiting the sick, and after that a call at one of the neighbouring factories where he talked to the men during their dinner hour. The afternoon was devoted to house-to-house visiting, and the evening commenced with an open-air meeting at a street corner, opposite the public house, to be followed by an after-meeting at the Mission Hall.

As the years passed the work changed and became far more varied, as this account of a parish in 1922 indicates.

> The Vicar says: "Here you are, Captain, and here is your district. Go ahead, and God's blessing be upon your efforts." The prospect is not bright; a broken-down building in a slum, people frankly indifferent, sometimes hostile. He must first gain their confidence. He soon becomes a familiar figure; in and out of the houses he moves, bright and cheerful, bringing with him comfort and consolation in trouble and sorrow, advice in time of difficulty, help in time of need. He chums up with the men, enters into their sports and recreations, and discusses with them the various problems that agitate their minds. He also makes friends with the young people, and often his success in this direction lays the foundation for successful work with the older people, reaching the hearts of the parents through their children.
>
> While he is gaining the confidence of the people he is also organizing and carrying out a definite aggressive Evangelistic Mission. He will select a street and go from house to house announcing that on that evening he will hold a service for them in the street. If he can secure the help of others, he does so, and a bright simple service is held. The people

may be shy and stand afar off, or they may not appear at all, but nevertheless they listen behind doors and windows while the message of God's love is delivered, and though there may be apparent indifference, he knows that many have heard who never enter a place of worship. Sometimes this open air effort takes the form of a lantern service, and much interest is aroused by the sacred pictures which convey through the eye the truths the Captain endeavours to teach.

The outdoor efforts are the prelude to an attempt to secure attendance at the mission hall or church. These services are usually of a very simple character; sometimes they take the form of a shortened evensong and gradually get the people accustomed to the Church service. A great point is made of the early Sunday morning Celebration of the Holy Communion, and it is usual for the Captain and his mission people to assemble half an hour before the time for a short prayer meeting, and then to proceed to the parish Church for Holy Communion.

Many flourishing churches have owed their success to the work of a captain like this one, and, though he would undoubtedly meet with discouragements, he would have the joy of seeing men and women awaken to their need of God, and find a source of peace, joy and power in their lives.

Today, like his predecessor, the Church Army captain may share in the whole parish ministry, taking part in many of the ordinary parochial activities and also seizing opportunities for communicating the Gospel to the people. But, with the present shortage of clergy, he may often be the officer in charge of a daughter or mission church; or he may have some special task, such as organizing the youth work in a large parish or for a group of churches.

In the case of the sisters, it has always been more difficult to separate the parochial from the social work. The earliest parochial workers were known as "mission nurses" for, at a time when medical attention was rarely available for the poor, much of their work lay in caring for the sick and the infirm.

A day's work of a mission nurse in the East India docks

in 1902 started with a visit to the rectory to get relief for
one or two sick people, and to a nursing sister of St. John
the Divine for a surgical instrument and some convales-
cent home letters; then on to the draper's to buy various
prints and flannelettes for the mothers' meeting. After
dinner she visited in her area, and this involved cleaning
and tidying up for those who were ill, the dressing of
wounds, and the comforting of some in trouble. As one
harassed mother remarked: "Yer can open your heart to
them as knows what beats yer." Later in the evening was
a mission service for girls, and help for a blind man who
had stumbled into the service.

The need for much of this home nursing ceased when
more district nurses were trained, and in 1906 the "mission nurse" became the "mission sister". She now had
more time for parish work, and would run the mothers'
meeting or the women's club, help with the guides or
brownies, or organize a girls' club. She might be needed
for the lantern service, or as organist, and her home
would be open to all who liked to come and was often the
centre where small groups gathered. In her spare time she
would distribute the *Church Army Gazette*. This gave her
the chance for an introduction to people whom she might
not otherwise meet, and of hearing of those in trouble or
ill.

Nowadays the work of the Church Army sister is much
wider in scope. In addition to her ordinary parochial activities of visiting the sick and the old and teaching the
children, she may, like the Church Army sister in one of
the older towns, be called upon to be chairman of the Old
People's Welfare Committee, acting padre of the Toc H
Women's Association, a frequent speaker at Mothers'
Union meetings, and an organizer of working parties in
connexion with the headquarters needlework guild.

Church Army captains and sisters have often been sent
to housing estates and new towns, for the people who
move into them can be very bewildered at first, find it

C

difficult to settle down, and feel a need for something beyond themselves. A new house, a new town, amongst new people can be a very good reason for a new beginning.

The Cedars Estate, belonging to the London County Council, with some 1,300 houses lying west of Harrow Weald, is a typical example.

> The residents arrived in 1948 from various parts of London and at once found themselves busy arranging their homes— an unaccustomed privilege for many—and wrestling with the rough gardens. The increase in travelling time for many of the men meant that they did not see their homes in daylight from October until April, except at weekends. The residents had little time for outside activities and even less opportunity, for the estate consisted exclusively of houses and a few shops. There was no church, no church youth club or Sunday school, and the few worshippers who attended churches outside the area felt they "did not belong". By the time the incumbent of the enormous parish secured a Church Army worker for the estate, any public desire for such help seemed to have died out.

When the Church Army captain did arrive in 1950, he adopted a policy which has proved successful in many similar situations. This was to concentrate first on the youth. In the early summer a youth church was opened in the day school and this was attended by a handful of young people. Hymns and Church Army choruses formed an integral part of the service, with a ten minute address or a group discussion. Several months later a youth club was formed which placed emphasis on the service of others. Old people were visited and those who could come to the hall were entertained with country dancing and singing. Then the homes of the parents were tackled, and many of them were opened to the Church Army captain as a result of his friendship with the children. A young wives' group was the next to be formed, and from these beginnings church congregations began to grow, Sunday school to be attended, and people to offer themselves for Christian service.

In the new towns there is always the difficulty of starting from scratch. In one of these, the vicar and captain visited every family when it arrived, with offers of help with moving in, decorating, and settling down. Thus, contact was made with the people at once, before they had time to form other interests. A builders' hut was used for services until the new church could be built, and many who had rarely been to church before started to come.

These are only a few examples of the ways in which a Church Army captain or sister can help an incumbent as a member of his staff. In practice, there are many variants depending upon the personal abilities of the officer, and the needs of the people in the district. No means are too difficult or trivial if the captain is to reach the people among whom he lives and works, and, like Wilson Carlile, he is ready to use whatever things come to hand. But he is always under the authority of the vicar of the parish, and the ultimate decision as to the forms of work which he undertakes and the methods which he uses is the decision of the incumbent. The captain or sister stays in a parish as long as he or she is needed, and when this is no longer the case, headquarters will place them in some other Church Army work.

THE EVANGELISTIC MISSION

Sometimes Church Army officers will be invited to a parish for a short length of time, usually to conduct a mission. Such missions have always formed an important part of Church Army work, and at first they were held by individual evangelists, or "pioneers" as they were called. On the request of the vicar, a "pioneer" would be sent by headquarters to conduct a mission in his parish. He would take his tent with him, and pitch it on a piece of open ground, and it would serve both as the mission centre and as his own living quarters. Meetings would be held outside, in the open, and at other times the men could come and sit and smoke with him inside the tent. Working men who had little use for the conventional forms of Christianity would often be attracted in this way.

Sometimes a larger mission was required, and so united missions were started, covering several parishes and including a variety of types of churchmanship. They would last about ten days, starting on a Saturday with an introductory service at one of the churches and an address by the bishop of the diocese. The evangelists, with the clergy and congregation, would then march to some large hall where a mass meeting would be held. On Sunday the mission services would begin in the hall, and Wilson Carlile would often manage to be present. There would be weekday meetings during the dinner hour in the factories, and women and children's meetings in the afternoons. But the main mission service would be in the evening with a full choir, wind instruments, and probably the help of the magic lantern.

Such missions were especially popular in the early twenties in the industrial areas, where they were held in many of the large towns. The press, describing the "laughing crusaders at Bootle", tells how a

score of missioners were welcomed by the Bishop of Liverpool and solemnly set apart for their task. This reception service was followed by a magnificent procession of witness, nearly 1,000 persons taking part. The Bishop of Liverpool, the Mayor and Mayoress of Bootle, and Prebendary Carlile took the lead, supported by noted clergy and choristers; and the St. Helen's Church Army band provided the music. The popular inaugural gathering was held in the spacious hall of the Linacre Mission, and, though it seats 1,500, many had to stand. Clergy taking part in the mission occupied each of the church pulpits on the Sunday. Captain Hanson, the chief lay missioner, quickly got to grips with 1,000 men on the first Sunday afternoon and 1,500 on the second Sunday afternoon in the Metropole Theatre. The week-end gatherings were held in the Town Hall, and a great company gathered night by night to hear Captain Hanson. Already arrangements are being made for a return visit to Bootle.

The value of these missions lay not only in the fact that they promoted unity between the churches in an area, and added to the number of churchgoers and confirmation candidates in the parishes, but also that they helped to interpret God to many people who had only the vaguest ideas about Him.

Similar missions were held in the 1950's in the form of deanery or diocesan missions, and were much favoured by Edward Wilson Carlile during his period as chief secretary. Like his grandfather, he was keenly interested in new and improved methods of evangelism, and in introducing some of the modern group principles which were being used in other spheres. The evangelists would work as a team, each member knowing exactly how to fit in with the others on any occasion. This was made possible by the far greater and earlier preparation that was now carried on for such missions. The area would be visited a year or so beforehand, and plans made well in advance. Groups in the parish would be asked to talk and pray about the coming mission, so that an air of expectancy was created by the time that the missioners arrived. Many more meetings would be held in people's homes, and would be of a less formal nature. Questions would be encouraged on a wide variety of subjects, and the mobile daylight cinema would tour the parishes to show modern Christian films.

Today there is a return to the parish mission, perhaps because the needs of the modern world are becoming more personal and intimate. The so-called "Flying Columns" of evangelists help by being ready at any time to respond to the call of a vicar. First formed in the early fifties, the Flying Column consisted of a team of three captains and a sister which operated from London, and visited different parishes throughout the country. It conducted between fifteen and twenty missions in a year, and the fact that it travelled some 1,000 miles each month brought it into contact with an astonishingly large number of people. Soon the number of evangelists was increased to six, and its success led to the formation of two other motorized teams—the Midland Mobile Mission, or M.M.M. as it is familiarly called, and the Northern Evangelistic Team, or the N.E.T., with its centre at Manchester.

As well as these groups, many of the dioceses now have area team evangelists, both captains and sisters, who can be sent to parishes to lead missions when these are wanted. Their programmes are adapted to fit the particular needs of each parish, and are carefully prepared beforehand. Home meetings, to which church people invite their neighbours, are especially encouraged, and the Gospel is preached through the discussion of everyday problems rather than by direct teaching. Thus in a new way it is hoped to reach the people who never come to church, and who know little about the meaning of Christianity.

TOURING THE COUNTRYSIDE

As Wilson Carlile soon found out, the ordinary parochial worker and the parish missions rarely touched the people living in the country. So following the precedent of other country missions, he started to use a caravan to take the evangelists from one village to another. It was on June 24, 1892, that the first Church Army mission van, with Captain Prior in charge, set off from headquarters down the Edgware Road to visit the countryside south of London. It was not easy at first, for in those days prejudice and misconception made many of the clergy look askance at such an innovation, and it was a strict rule that the van would only stop in a parish where it was invited to do so by the incumbent. But gradually the clergy were won over by the success which was achieved, and within ten years the vans were acceptable in most rural parishes.

A contemporary writer describes how

> the entry of the van into a great country parish is in itself
> something of a novelty, being very conspicuous with its
> striking texts of scripture painted in white on a dark green
> ground. The mission consists in holding services in the
> school, church or other available place. Meetings take place
> in the open air, on the village green, market square, or out-
> side large works, preceded by house visitation. The service
> itself consists of a few hymns, a few collects, a lesson and a
> plain and simple Gospel address. A strange face, a fresh
> voice, new methods adopted in a special effort of this kind,
> all combine to direct the attention of the careless and the
> indifferent.

Life was not easy for workers on these mission vans.
There was never a great deal of room for the three or four
occupants. In the winter the vans could be extremely cold,
and in the summer very hot. But the Church Army workers
were always busy with breakfast and dinner-hour services
for working people, afternoon gatherings for women, after-
tea meetings for children, and an open-air procession and
a big indoor meeting in the evening, as well as their own
regular devotions and study. Like the Franciscans, they
had to "beg" their way, for although the Church Army
paid their salaries, working costs had to be defrayed by the
people of the parishes through which they passed, and this
included the hire of horses when they moved from one
parish to another, and their own food and other personal
needs. Sometimes a friendly farmer lent them a horse, and
gifts of food or hospitality were often provided.

During the first world war these van missions would
have ceased had it not been for the sisters in the Lichfield
and St. Albans dioceses, who carried on the work. Not
everyone approved of this, but the Church Army has always been of the opinion that mission work should be done
by both men and women. With women in charge of a van,
however, there were fewer open-air meetings and big
gatherings, but more cottage meetings and house-to-house

visiting. This helped to provide the personal touch, which
is often absent in travelling mission work. Since then,
sisters have continued to work with the vans, travelling
over the countryside in pairs; and with the use of motor
vans, which were introduced in 1922, their work has become a little less heavy.

Very cosy indeed are these vans. Though sleeping there
all through the wild winter nights, in the daytime they
manage so to pack up the beds that the whole length of the
van is available, and the end of the van makes a sort of cosy
corner, with the cushions which are pillows at night. A little
fold-up table in the centre, gives plenty of room for three to
partake of a meal, or for writing and accounts. An oil lamp
gives not only light, but also heat, and the little stove boils
the ever-ready kettle very efficiently. In these country
places, the visit of a van is a tremendous spiritual asset, and
the vicars are very glad to welcome the sisters.

The vans were frequently used for work among people
who did not fit into the ordinary life of a parish. For
example, at Moreton in Cheshire in the early twenties, the
vicar was worried about the colonies of one-roomed caravans housing families working in Birkenhead or Liverpool,
or living on the dole or a disability pension. The Chester
diocesan van, manned by two captains, was parked for a
time in the middle of one of these colonies. The captains
were thus able to get to know the people intimately, and as
there was no meeting hall, they invited them in small
groups to meetings in their caravan. People came more
readily than to a more formal meeting, and several eventually became linked with the church.

The vans were particularly useful for contacting people
such as gipsies or hop-pickers who stayed only a short time
in one place. In 1933, in the Winchester diocese, it was
stated:

the latest addition to our fleet of vans is to be used exclusively among the gipsies of the New Forest, a "parish' of
nearly one thousand souls, living in tents, selling pigs, bee-

hives and baskets; or getting a scant living in the fruit-orchards or hop-fields. These people are spiritually isolated, since their method of life makes them unwelcome in many ordinary Church congregations. There are many, however, who welcome the visits to their encampments of the Church Army Captains.

The captain found that the best plan was to park the van in one of the Forest villages, and to cycle round to the various little camps. He would collect the children and teach them all he could, and then invite the men and women to the services. The lantern shows were a great attraction, for the gipsies could rarely read or write but they understood this simple method of present-ation.

Today, vans manned by captains work in several of the English and Irish dioceses, with sisters' vans in three of them. A captain writes from the Leicester Diocesan Mission Van:

The initial approach to clergy is generally through a chapter meeting followed by personal contact. Then comes the opportunity of talking with the Parochial Church Council and possibly illustrating the work of the caravan team with a few coloured slides. If the P.C.C. decide later that it is right for a mission to take place, then some kind of preparation is encouraged. Unfortunately, however, this is often thought unnecessary, but usually serves some purpose by making ordinary church members aware that there is more to being a Christian than belonging to the Mothers' Union or Men's Group and going to church on Sunday. When the caravan eventually arrives in some prominent place in a village it usually creates quite a stir. Being seen around is usually a good advertisement that the mission is about to begin. Unless the mission is to have an emphasis on youth or children, then the programme caters for the needs of all age groups. Details are usually neatly presented in an attractive programme cover. The commissioning of the team to work in a parish is the signal for the prepared activities to get under way.

THE SUMMER CRUSADES

During the summer months the Church Army has for many years organized crusades from some cathedral city to the holiday resorts. These can trace their origin to the seaside missions, which were started in the nineties and were held at favoured resorts such as Southend and Blackpool. A contemporary account describes how a pioneer missioner, with a band of helpers, would invite the crowds to an open-air service, at which he would illustrate his talk with limelight pictures thrown on to a sheet in front of the people. Invitations would then be given for the tent service, and as the writer so truly says:

Men and women can be persuaded to enter that church when every effort to induce them to enter the parish church is fruitless, whilst a sudden shower will quickly cause the tent to be thronged.

By the time of the first world war there were eight of these seaside missions, but hostilities forced them to close, and after the war it was decided to incorporate them in a bigger scheme of summer crusades. These were based on the pattern of the war-time route march. Captains and sisters would gather at some cathedral city conveniently placed for several seaside resorts, and, after a send-off by the bishop and clergy, they would start treking slowly through the countryside, stopping at towns and villages on the way until after five or six weeks they reached their destination.

These Marching Crusades, as they were called, roused much interest as they passed along. A red banner with the words "Church Army Route March" would be carried at the head of each group, and behind would come the trek cart laden with kit bags and other needs. They would usually march in the morning, arrive at a village for lunch, and stay there for the rest of the day, visiting and taking meetings, if the vicar allowed. Their arrival was not entirely fortuitous, for the leader of each party would have cycled over the route earlier in the year, making arrangements as to where they would stop, and fixing for two nights' stay at the weekend, when they would often be invited to preach in the church or help in the Sunday school. Heralded by their banner, they would eventually arrive at their seaside destination, to begin a three or four weeks' mission.

Last Sunday was the first Sunday of the Church Army Crusade in Margate this year (1933). They had come on foot from York, where they were blessed and dismissed for the Crusade by the Archbishop. During the weeks following they had "tramped it" down England, teaching and preaching and receiving, as the Captain laughingly explained, "more board than lodging"—for accommodation is only possible in the form of a shake-down on the floors of the Church Schools—and a very large measure of kindness from clergy and Church people.

I watched the crowd as the service began. There was full Church witness in the service, the use of the Creed, the Our Father, the Collects and the simple and better-known prayers and petitions. There were hymns and short addresses. I had expected some of the loungers to move away. No one did. Mothers continued to feed their babies from medicine bottles of milk. Some cyclists, propped up against the promenade wall, openly joined in the service. Fathers woke up, were frankly bored with the hymns, but listened to hear, in the short explanations, who each Church Army man was, what work he had done in factory, workshop or trade, and why he was there to give testimony to the truth of the Gospel and of the Church. For men are mostly interested if they start with some common knowledge of and understanding with the speaker. The promenade railing had a tightly-packed line of listeners, who looked down at the service below them on the sands.

When the second world war ended, the crusaders set out once more, but the time they could spend was shortened, so cycles and public transport might be used, or a motorized team would start from a more distant destination. Eight teams left Durham on July 4, 1955, for Clee-thorpes, Bridlington, Swansea, New Brighton, Blackpool, Great Yarmouth, Hastings and Lowestoft, and, since they had to arrive at their destinations by the beginning of August, they could not do the journey entirely on foot. By 1963 the Crusade was almost entirely motorized, with cars, trailers, motor cycles, a Land Rover, and some of the men's vans. It was hard to believe that only in 1953 a sister could write "our shortest walk was eighteen miles", and that in 1958 teams of officers had marched from Winchester Cathedral pulling the bright red trek carts.

At the seaside, too, things have changed. Open-air services on the beach and in the town are still important, but acting, conjuring and quizzes are mingled with straight-forward preaching. A church hall is usually the head-quarters of the mission, where all the arrangements are made. The captains and students often sleep there, and all assemble there for their midday meal, taking their turns in preparing it. One sister wrote home to her family: "Everything is going well so far. The men's cooking is quite good." Members of the team are invited to do a wide range of things. Some speak at Sunday services in the local churches. Hospitals and old people's homes are visited, and the housebound called upon. But it is still the children who receive the main impact of the mission, and for whom games are arranged, services held and excursions planned.

CHILDREN'S MISSIONS

Special work for children, not only at the seaside, was started in the early years of the last war, when many children were evacuated or away from their homes and so might be out of touch with Christian influence. It began in the Liverpool diocese, when two Church Army sisters were invited to come as children's missioners. By 1947 the

Church Army had decided that this should form an integral part of their work, and by 1950 children's missions were taking place in many parishes.

They are intended primarily to help the children of church people, but it is hoped that those outside the reach of any Sunday school or church will be attracted as well. They are essentially teaching missions and use all the modern aids that can be procured. The sisters who lead them are qualified in teaching children and seize every opportunity of exploring and practising modern methods of communication, such as visual aids, models, charts, flannelgraphs and other pictorial ways of putting across their message.

The mission starts when a town or parish invites the Church Army to send a "team", which usually consists of two sisters, who have been trained for the work, with perhaps a sister in training. After preliminary consultation with the clergy, a meeting is announced to which people especially concerned with children's work, are invited. Advance publicity of a contemporary nature plays a big part in ensuring full meetings and services.

A rather novel attraction was used to precede a mission at St. Peter's with St. Aidan's, Balkwell (North Shields), when space-ships dominated posters and programmes. There were space-ships everywhere and the largest and most colourful was on the parish church itself which was floodlit. On the official launching date the children all came out of school to hear the music of "I wish I was a space-man!"

The children are not told about the mission far ahead, though the sisters sometimes like to meet them a few days beforehand, as they are very good recruiting agents. The mission usually lasts for eight days, Sunday to Sunday, and on the first Sunday the missioners are commissioned, often by a visiting clergyman. During the week two or three meetings of different age groups are held in the afternoons or early evenings. The children in the under-eight groups are mostly accompanied by one of their parents. In the eight-to-eleven group and the eleven plus they come on their own and engage in a variety of activities both as teams and individually. Nothing is greater fun than the inevitable "do-it-yourself", and they make their own prayer books, scrap books to give away to the hospitals, and design and paint calendars and birthday books. The prayer request box gets surprisingly full with many original requests. A sister, one day, found a slip of paper in the box, asking for a prayer to be said for "a poorly Beatle".

Every child who attends the mission has an attendance card, and from this card the parish is given a detachable slip with the child's name, address and age, so that after the mission contact may be maintained. Newcomers to the church are invited to join the Sunday school, and children who have taken a leading part in the mission are encouraged to help with other church activities.

Although the mission is directed to the children, interest centres on the whole family. Thus, on the second Sunday of the mission, the children are invited to bring their parents to Evensong, and many who would otherwise never go to church may come to this. Mothers who bring their younger children to the meetings often stay to help with what they are doing, and they have a special evening meeting of their own when they can discuss their children's problems. For many adults the children's mission may be a turning-point in their lives, and the final service is as packed with them as it is with children.

Sometimes a Church Army officer is asked to become a children's adviser in a diocese. This has happened in Peterborough and Southwell, where a captain and a sister respectively now help to arrange the work. For Sunday school children there are short holiday courses, with the opportunity of taking the Inter-diocesan Children's Examination set by the Church of England Children's Council. For school leavers, day conferences are held on subjects like "Learning and Earning", including such aspects as "Why we choose a job", "How to behave at an interview" and "The use of leisure". There is also a special course for mentally handicapped children. Those who help with these courses are trained in the use of the latest Sunday school lesson books, expression work material and visual aids. Thus many lay people are brought into this form of evangelistic work, and bring their special talents to it.

TRAINING THE LAITY

Wilson Carlile was always emphatic that evangelism should not be left to trained evangelists, but that all Christian people should be encouraged to help. One of his great rallying cries was "Every communicant an evangelist". It was members of his own congregation who accompanied him into the streets and supported him at the open-air meetings in Kensington, and later, when Rector of St. Mary-at-Hill, he expected his church members to accompany him to the open-air meetings in Petticoat Lane and Spitalfields churchyard. Similarly, when conducting missions throughout the country, church members were always encouraged to take a leading part and to form a permanent evangelistic group when the mission was over. In fact, in the very early days, there were both Church Army officers and soldiers, the latter being people who, though not enrolled members of the Church Army, were ready to take part in evangelistic missions on Church Army lines wherever they happened to live or work.

Some sort of training was obviously necessary if the laity were to become effective evangelists, and so in March 1923 Wilson Carlile decided to hold an evangelistic week-end for Church workers at the training college, and from that date such week-ends formed an important part of Church Army activities. They were attended by men and women from all walks of life, with a good sprinkling of students and ordinands. Evangelism was not merely explained

and discussed, but all were expected to take an active
part.

"Follow me—and I will make you to become fishers of
men!" It was this call that brought about fifty young women,
from all parts of the country, to Church Army Headquarters one week-end in September 1956. Each had heard
the call to serve Our Lord by personal witness—to join in
the work of evangelism. But how does one set about this—
what is evangelism? Well, that is what brought us all to
London. Our first session on evangelism came after lunch,
when we gathered for "Call to Service". One by one, we
stood up and told how we had come to know Jesus—how we
were daily proving his power in our lives. There were several
other opportunities of speaking for our Lord. The most
thrilling were at the Hyde Park open-air meetings on
Saturday and Sunday evening. How often we have laughed
at jokes about "soap-box spouters" in Hyde Park, little
realizing that one day we too would earn that title! These
meetings were followed by Lantern Services in the Headquarters Chapel—but first we had a chance to try "fishing".
This meant standing in Edgware Road and inviting
passers-by to come into our service. Then, in Chapel, as the
pictures were flashed on the screen, we spoke as the Holy
Spirit put a message in our hearts. There was hymn-singing
too, and, at the end, a chance for personal talks with those
who had accepted our invitation to "come and join us".

During the week-end we also had an insight into the
'social' evangelism of the Church Army. Instead of going to
the Chapel service on Saturday evening, several of us
visited Bethany, a flat at Headquarters. Earlier in the afternoon, we heard about moral welfare work. Then on the
Sunday morning we visited Church Army hostels. One of
the great joys of Christianity is fellowship and we certainly
experienced this during the week-end. The week-end was
over all too soon and we returned to our various walks of
life. What difference was our experience of evangelism going
to make in the many parishes represented at Headquarters?

So wrote a visitor in 1956. Evangelistic week-ends are still
held, and students from theological colleges, doctors pre-

paring for overseas missionary work, teachers, engineers, and people from many different walks of life are among those who come as the Church Army guests.

In the mid-thirties a new type of lay evangelism was started in the form of the "News Team". There was a growing concern throughout the Church about the need for evangelism. *Recall to Religion* had been issued by the Archbishop of Canterbury, with the challenge that "there ought certainly to be in almost every parish, teams within that parish who can be the living witness". Wilson Carlile had himself conducted a series of "World Call" services in cathedrals and parish churches in which he appealed to Church members to renew their baptismal and confirmation vows and to go out and spread the message of Christianity. Therefore he suggested that news teams of lay people within the parishes should be specially trained for this purpose, and the first of these was formed in July, 1934.

Each team was to consist of six to twenty members, chosen by the vicar from among the younger people of his congregation. The object was to constitute a group whose varied and contrasting experiences of Christian living, simply and sincerely told, would relate the power of the Gospel to a varied audience. The team was under lay leadership, the Church Army instructions being that the leader "does not preach, but introduces the witnesses as a chairman does, and keeps to time. He should know all their trades, jobs and abodes. He should have a good smile and a sense of humour." Within the parish the team stood ready for anything—visiting in the new housing estates, cottage and drawing-room meetings, fellowship groups and study circles. But their big occasion was the "Guest Night", when they went to some other parish to speak at a large meeting, composed principally of non-church-goers.

It was a guest night which I attended, and the Team in this instance came from Watford. They numbered, with their leader, eight. They had many difficulties to contend with; a depressing mission hall, a mixed crowd none too easy

D

to hold, and a great deal of noise from outside. But in a service entirely devoid of trimmings, and devoted exclusively to witness, they put their news over in a way that stirred their hearers deeply and moved many of them to decision. It was all thoroughly natural and unforced. The speakers were neither self-conscious nor artificially hearty. They each had something worth hearing to say, and they said it without waste of words or of time—eight simple testimonies, but they changed the whole atmosphere of the place.

Often a news team was formed first as part of a Church Army mission to a parish, to provide the nucleus of active mission workers. It would consist of people willing to take responsibility by prayer, work and witness. With that intention they would undertake Bible study, train to visit the homes of the parish, encourage others to join them, arrange home meetings, and in all ways seek to prepare their parish for the mission itself. After the mission was over, the news team would help with the follow-up, welcoming those won by the mission into the fellowship of the Church, and helping them at the beginning of their Christian life. Some dioceses would commission news team evangelists to organize their mission work; in others, they might be invited to come for short periods from headquarters. By August 1939, five hundred news teams were in action in Britain with a staff of thirty-five news team officers. During the war over sixty news teams of church people were conducting short epilogues in the large air-raid shelters, particularly those in the underground stations in London.

After the war the news teams continued, but they did not recapture the spontaneity and enthusiasm of pre-war days. It was therefore decided to let them lapse, and to look for some new method which would take into account the different outlook of the post-war period. "Christian Advance" was substituted for the news teams in 1960, not just to give them another name, but to try to adapt evangelism to modern ways of thought.

Its main task is "to help the man in the pew to think seriously about the secular world, from God's viewpoint; to look on his work as his main calling in life, and not as an unhappy interruption to running some church club, or making things for the annual bazaar". "Stewardship" is perhaps the key word to this, but interpreted not merely in terms of money but in forms of service, particularly in evangelism.

Christian Advance programmes usually start with a conference of Church Army officers and lay people, at which informal discussions take place on such subjects as "What is the church in my parish doing?", "What is the purpose of the Church?", "What is man's basic need?" Then, if the group decide to undertake further training they are supplied with the training leaflets which are intended to be used at the different sessions. A full course should make the participants aware of their responsibilities as Church members, able to meet each other as people, and ready to get on with the job of introducing men and women to Christ.

THE PARAPHERNALIA OF EVANGELISM

Thus, in its varied forms of evangelism, the Church Army has always sought to adapt itself to the needs of the moment. "How to reach the masses?" was a question continually on the lips of Wilson Carlile, and he answered it in a variety of ways which changed according to the particular circumstances of the prevailing situation. But the one principle to which he paid great attention was to produce something arresting which would cause a person to stop and inquire what was going on. Processions, banners, a trombone or a cornet, an alluring newspaper, pictures on a screen, a mobile cinema, were all part of the paraphernalia of evangelism—"gimmicks, gimmicks, gimmicks", as they were irreverently called at a recent concert at the Church Army training college.

One of the old-fashioned "gimmicks" was the *Church Army Gazette*, which was only one year younger than the Church Army itself, the first number being dated April 2, 1883. In its early days it had many contributors and several editors, among them Wilson Carlile himself, but eventually it passed into the hands of Mary Burn, who, gauging her public with a nicety, knew exactly what they wanted.

> So the little paper girdles the globe. To working men and women all over the world, to village and slum, to ships and barracks, prisons, hospitals, workhouse and lodging-house —to all, by various channels, it finds its way, and wherever it goes it is read. Peeping over a reader's shoulder one easily sees why. For it is what the Americans call a live paper. The clergyman who writes the football story is evidently a keen player; the Animals' Hospital is described by a real lover of animals; the Cup Final and King Edward's funeral were specially reported by an eye-witness. Cricket, football, roller-skating, aeroplanes, town planning, books, gardening, poultry, domestic matters, combine to fill it chock full of human interest.

This was 1910, when the weekly circulation had reached about 113,000 copies.

Nearly the whole of each issue was sold for a halfpenny from door to door. In most cases the captains and sisters were assisted by large numbers of voluntary helpers, banded together as Gazette Brigades. In some towns the captains sold the *Gazette* in public houses, and then it often provided means of getting into touch with a person who would not otherwise be approached. Another distributing agency was the Greater Britain Gazette Brigade, managed by a lady of eighty-seven, who posted copies to subscribers abroad. Not only was it "a means of stating the Christian Gospel in ordinary everyday language and of giving the younger and the adult members of the family something which will make them think of God's claim on their lives", but it also made considerable yearly profits which were devoted to the work of the Church Army.

In the years before the two wars it still sold some 80,000 copies per week, and though its character had changed, it met the needs of a variety of people.

> A doctor wants a Christian paper for his surgery table; a team of young people want to undertake regular visiting in the parish, distributing Christian literature; a Christian magazine is required for a women's meeting; some Church members, following a mission, want to take their faith into the pubs and clubs of the parish.

But after the second world war there was not the same desire for this type of newspaper. It was, therefore, decided in January, 1962, to cease publication. Instead, the *Spearhead* takes its place as a quarterly magazine of evangelism appealing especially to the younger people in the Church.

In order to print the *Gazette*, Wilson Carlile had acquired a printing press, housed in some ramshackle cottages in Salisbury Mews. Miss Burn writes:

> In those days we were too poor to have many original pictures drawn and made into blocks, so we used to buy ready-made pictures and write editorials to fit them. . . . On one occasion the man in the picture had a wooden leg, and the man in the story obviously had not, so it was questioned whether to alter the picture to fit the story or the story to fit the picture.

Booklets, handbills, stationery and circulars were also printed there, and it soon became apparent that more commodious and up-to-date premises should be secured. An anonymous letter appeared in *The Guardian* in 1903 which said that in memory of a beloved only son his heirs wished to devote his printing works to the service of mankind. Negotiations were opened with the writer and as a result the printing works at Cowley, Oxford, were offered to the Church Army, rent free. Here, for many years the *Gazette* and other publications of the Church Army were printed, with the help of labour from the social departments but under ordinary working conditions and trade union regulations. The increased use of the printing works by Church societies, commerical firms, local authorities, hospital boards, and the general public, made it necessary not only to install up-to-date modern equipment, but also to extend the building itself. This was done in 1964, when a new building was erected to connect the machine-room and the bindery and so to increase the speed of delivery.

Two other requirements of a Church Army evangelist in the early days were a banner and a magic lantern. At every open-air meeting the Church Army banner was displayed and was the inevitable target for showers of rotten eggs, flour and red ochre which were the usual accompaniments of outdoor meetings. If the banner could be brought down it was a great achievement for the hooligans.

The first banners were the work of friends of the Church Army, but soon a banner and art department was started to make banners and altar cloths, not only for their outdoor work and small chapels, but to supply the needs of other churches as well. This often formed useful employment for the more educated woman who was out of a job, and many of these helped in the workroom at headquarters. The tradition of fine needlework and embroidery is still carried on by a sister in the Church Army Embroidery Room, where the needs both of the Church Army and of other organizations, such as the Mothers' Union, are supplied.

The magic lantern played a great part for it could be used at all indoor meetings and served as a strong enticement to those who were not at all interested in religion. Wilson Carlile had only to advertise a lantern show, and his hall was filled to capacity with people who would never dream of coming to church. The Church Army Lantern Department can be said to date from 1882, when Miss Cheshire began to keep a few slides in a cupboard to lend out to Church Army evangelists. Very soon others wanted to borrow these slides, and a thriving business was started in making and selling slides for the clergy, missionaries and other members of the public, on an upper floor at 14 Edgware Road.

When the lantern became out of date it was replaced by the cinematograph, and the Lantern and Cinema Department added projectors and filmstrips to its stock. In 1952 the department had five filmstrips in its catalogue; five years later it had eight hundred.

A new and important development in evangelistic work is the tape recorder. Many churches find it particularly useful in taking the service to the people, especially to those who are old or housebound, in hospital, or in isolated and widely scattered places.

The equipment for these different forms of visual-aid, which are now so widely used in teaching, is all to be found in the visual-aid department, which has not only over a thousand titles in its *Filmstrips for the Church*, but sells projectors, screens, tape records, records and record players, photographic supplies, "Letraset" instant lettering and many other requirements for making the Gospel appeal to an audience. Captains and sisters use them a great deal and find them invaluable, not only in teaching children, but in prisons and other institutions where what is seen is often of more significance than what is heard.

From April, 1947, until quite recently the mobile daylight cinema van took films all over the country, giving shows in streets, hop-fields, school playgrounds, dockyards, factories, seaside resorts, and on open spaces and bomb sites. It was one of the most successful instruments of evangelism which the Church Army possessed, for it attracted people who would never think of attending a religious meeting. Its lunch-hour services in factory, mining and dock areas drew large numbers of men who would gather round to watch and listen for the whole of their break from work.

Books might seem out of date with this increase in modern methods of communication, but the bookshop on the ground floor of 185 Marylebone Road, does not find that this is so. The earliest bookshop of the Church Army was the mission van, and for several years books were obtained from a City firm and sold in this way. Captains and sisters needed books, especially cheap reprints of standard works, if they were to keep up the quality of their talks and sermons. Therefore a bookroom was opened in an upstairs room in the headquarters at 130 Edgware Road and later at 14 Edgware Road. It was not until 1948 that the ground floor shop at number 14 could be used, and then for the first time it was possible to serve the general public. Sales began to increase, and continued when the bookshop was moved to 55 Bryanston Street, and later to 185 Marylebone Road. When the plans for widening this road and building the new fly-over are completed, the present bookshop will be in a commanding position for both members of the Church Army and the increased number of passers-by.

In 1954 it was decided to co-ordinate the work of the bookshop, the visual-aid department and the printing works at Cowley in the form of the Church Army Press and Supplies Ltd., and so to give the advantages of incorporation to these business projects which concern both members of the Church Army and the general public.

The battle of evangelism, which the Church Army was formed to fight in 1882, continues. It is still being waged against the forces of indifference and unbelief, and its methods are still flexible and constantly adapted to meet changing needs. Sometimes they are successful, and sometimes they are not, but when existing methods seem to fail, something else is always tried. Though the Church Army is by no means the only group engaged in evangelism, it has the great advantage of being able to offer men and women who are fully trained and experienced to help the clergy who have little time for this type of work and are not expected to be particularly proficient in it.

CHAPTER III

The Social Work of the Church Army

IT WAS IN August 1882 that Wilson Carlile left the parish of St. Mary Abbots, Kensington, to start the evangelistic work which was soon to be known as the Church Army. In November, 1889, the first Church Army "Labour Home" was established in connexion with his evangelistic mission in Marylebone, and social work began. The *Annual Report* for 1939, which records the jubilee of the men's social department, states that

> this social work came through the attendance of cold, half-starved, ragged, destitute men attending a series of evangelistic meetings at St. Mary's Hall, Marylebone.

It is doubtful if Wilson Carlile had anticipated that much of the evangelism of the Church Army would be through their social work, and the fact that this happened was largely due to the economic conditions of the late nineteenth century. His intention had been to take Christianity to those who would never darken the door of a church and who were mostly to be found in the lower income groups, especially among the very poor. Differences in wealth were much more marked than they are today, and Charles Booth, in his survey of *The Life and Labour of the People of London, 1891–1903*, reckoned that at least thirty per cent of the population were in poverty, and of these eight per cent were completely destitute.

As he went round among such people in North Kensington, Westminster, and later in Marylebone, Wilson Car-

lile found an indifference and a despair largely the result
of the appalling conditions in which they lived, and the
complete lack of security of income, and indeed of life itself. Their energies were almost entirely engaged in keeping body and soul together, and they associated religion
with wealth and comfort, as well they might, for few
churches would tolerate their presence. It was to people
like this that Wilson Carlile was determined to reveal the
love of God, and he soon found that they understood kindness and help in their difficulties far better than any
preaching. Care for them as individuals helped to restore
their self-confidence, and then it was possible to speak to
them about their spiritual needs.

The early years of Church Army social work were almost entirely occupied with helping the desperately poor,
and this general relief work brought to light some of the
special needs of the people who sought help. Many had
been in prison, and so care for ex-prisoners was started.
Drunkenness was widely prevalent, and so homes for inebriates were opened. Homeless children required care and
protection; and unmarried mothers, who were ostracized
by society, needed somewhere to live. Wherever some
special need became apparent attempts were made to
meet it.

The types of Church Army social work have changed as
the years have gone by, for needs have altered, methods
have improved, and the State has gradually taken over the
responsibility for an increasing number of these needs,
until today, with our welfare state, it is often felt that there
is little room for the social work of groups like the Church
Army. This is by no means the case, for the State recog-
nizes that it cannot supply the special needs of those whose
circumstances differ greatly from the majority. It is here
that societies like the Church Army have to take over, and
they do so, not only with a deep compassion for the less
fortunate but with a great longing that they may be able
to bring such people nearer to God.

THE HOMELESS AND DESTITUTE

Much of the work of the Church Army has been for the homeless and destitute. These can be found in any country, their numbers being usually related to the state of employment. There will always be poverty when there is insufficient work to go round, and this poverty will be more widespread in periods of trade depression. This happened in England from 1885–95, and again in the early years of the twentieth century. But the worst period of depression was from 1930–33 when there were nearly three million unemployed, many of them being out of work for several years. The Church Army always has a certain number of people in poverty to care for, but at times such as these, when emergency schemes have had to be introduced, its resources have been strained to the limit.

The Church Army started when there was great poverty and distress throughout the whole of Europe. Harvests were poor, winters were extremely cold, wages were low, accommodation was over-crowded and expensive in the towns, and employment extremely erratic. This was particularly the case in Germany when, after the Franco-German war, unemployed soldiers swarmed over the countryside, many of them almost completely destitute. The authorities were unable to cope with the situation, and so they gave support to various charitable organizations engaged in setting up labour colonies for such people. Pastor von Bodelschwingh's agricultural colony at Wilhelmsdorf, near Bielfeld, was perhaps the best known, for a popular account of it had been published in England, but many were also familiar with the Berlin colony which fed and sheltered many of the unemployed in that city.

Conditions in England were very similar at the end of the eighteen-eighties. The casual wards of the workhouses, which were intended to provide food and shelter for the homeless, were full, and many were forced to spend the night out, often crouching in doorways, huddling together in passages, or lying in the parks. The newspapers constantly contained accounts of those who died of exposure or starvation, and anyone who visited the poorer areas of the large towns would find ample confirmation of their truth. As on the continent, various voluntary societies, which provided food and shelter for the homeless, were doing their best to help, but even then only a small proportion of those in need were accommodated.

Therefore it is not surprising that both Wilson Carlile and General Booth of the Salvation Army, within a few months of one another, produced schemes for helping such people, and that these schemes were very similar, for they had, no doubt, both been inspired by the German experiments. Wilson Carlile outlined his methods in *Our Tramps*, produced early in 1890, and General Booth's ideas appeared in *In Darkest England and the Way Out*, published later in the year. They both envisaged labour colonies in the towns where the unemployed would be given work, agricultural colonies in a rural area where those who were suitable would be trained for work on the countryside, and overseas colonies to which those who were young enough for emigration would be sent. General Booth's scheme was far more pretentious and received much greater publicity, for he reckoned that his methods, if properly followed, would deal with all the distress throughout the country. Wilson Carlile had no intention of inaugurating such a widespread scheme, but primarily of helping the needy who came to the notice of the clergy in the different dioceses.

The first Church Army home was opened at 43 Crawford Street, off the Edgware Road, in 1890. It was known as the Tramps and Inebriates Home, and was described at the time as "a valuable addition to the work of the Society, enabling us to take men who would not work or who were out of work, and make them into 'working men' ". Wilson Carlile had hoped to establish similar homes in all the poorer parishes with financial help from the richer ones, but this never materialized, though by the end of the century there were seven of these labour homes in London and twenty in different provincial cities.

From the first, the Church Army was very careful as to whom it helped, and, unlike some societies, made a distinction between those who wanted to work, and those who were content to ask for charity. Men who came to the labour homes were questioned carefully when they arrived, and if in real need were given temporary help for the night with an hour's work after breakfast. If they still wished to stay they were given a three days' test and then a fortnight's continuous, steady work of eight hours a day with food and shelter. After that a contract of service was signed for four months, during which a regular wage was paid, and out of which the man was expected to meet his board and lodging. Then, if he were satisfactory, the Church Army found him a job.

It was not long before Wilson Carlile found it necessary to open lodging houses in connexion with some of the labour homes, both for those who had eventually obtained jobs and needed somewhere to live, and for other men who were unable to find cheap and respectable accommodation. The alternative was the common lodging house, and though some were reasonably clean, many were quite the opposite and frequented by most undesirable types. The Church Army lodging houses were not pretentious, but they did offer a man somewhere clean and cheap to live.

A visitor to any of our lodging houses will be welcomed by the Officer-in-charge and his wife. He will find clean floors and furniture, and fresh air; he will find cheerful, civil inmates, a good roaring fire, a nice reading room; he will find in some cases, as in Church Street, Marylebone, even a piano, and, I believe, performers! There are in the last named house, about fifty lodgers, some of whom have been there over a year.

Work in the labour homes was largely wood-chopping, and suitable for the older man and those not capable of learning a new form of occupation. The more promising ones were selected for agricultural training, and sent at first to Newdigate Farm in Surrey and then to Hempstead Hall in Essex.

> The object is to test the men's willingness to work, and to give them some elementary knowledge of farming before they go out to Canada. Some of the men are old soldiers, while a few have come down in the world through continued ill-fortune, and others are hooligans. All cannot learn milking; nor does it require many men to look after the number of horses that are kept; but digging, chaff-cutting, corn-grinding, and making hedges, supply plenty of work for willing hands.

This three-tiered scheme of labour homes and lodging houses, agricultural training and emigration lasted only a short while, for in 1907 the Canadian authorities changed their regulations, and although for a time men were sent to Australia and New Zealand, by 1910 farm training followed by emigration was confined to boys.

The first emergency scheme was started during the bad winter of 1903–4 when the Church Army was forced to make special arrangements for the unemployed. The end of the South Africa war and another period of trade depression led to an increase in the number of those with no settled home and no visible means of subsistence. Some were unemployable or incapable of keeping a job, either because they were untrained and or because they had been out of work for some time and had lost the desire or incentive to work. Many were married men with families who could not find a job locally and had tramped to London to try their luck there. This was a situation which was completely beyond the resources of the authorities.

Up to this time the Church Army had rejected the idea of night shelters for homeless men, on the grounds that adequate provision was made by others, and that such shelters only encouraged scroungers. But with these changed circumstances they came to the conclusion that the labour homes were insufficient to meet the situation, and that for the sake of men genuinely in need they must do something more to help. As was stated in an annual report:

> We face the fact that an enormous amount of unemployment and consequent suffering exists, and that relief cannot wait for the formulation and carrying into effect of vast schemes of social reform. Suffering must be dealt with on the spot, and we know of no better way to deal with it than by enabling the sufferer to earn honest wages, and not by offering gifts which must inevitably end in undermining self-respect and self-reliance, and in turning the unemployed into the unemployable.

An experiment was made in 1903, when one of the Church Army mission tents which had been erected in St. Thomas's churchyard, Westminster Bridge Road, was opened as a night shelter. Men were invited to come in and rest, and were given soup and bread. So many accepted the offer, and were obviously without any other accommodation, that it was decided to continue this work. But in future the unemployed men were to be given a job to do in return for their food and shelter.

In 1905, King Edward gave £100 to the Church Army towards its work for the destitute and the London County Council lent a piece of land, so that it became possible to erect what were called the King's labour tents.

> The men work in eight shifts of three hours each, one hundred men at a time, so that eight hundred can be, and generally are, received there every twenty-four hours. On beginning work they are fortified with nourishing soup, or cocoa and bread, for it was found that hunger had made many of them too weak to work. They then do their three hours' task of sawing, chopping or bundling wood, ready for sale; and afterwards are served with a good, hot, satisfying meal. When that is finished, each man is presented with a

ticket entitling him to a bed at a selected registered lodging house, so his elementary wants are satisfied for that day at least.

Then, as conditions grew worse, and men were obliged to wait several hours for employment in the King's tents, it was necessary to open another shelter, the Open-All-Night Shelter, for those who had tickets for employment but were not due to start work until 3 a.m. or 6 a.m.

Many of the unemployed, who were married men with children, were still trying to keep their homes going, but in order to do so were gradually forced to pawn or sell their possessions. The Queen's relief depots, which were supported by Queen Alexandra, were opened by the Church Army in different parts of London. Here the men were given a job and paid in cash, which, although it was only just sufficient to meet the needs of a family, at least enabled them to keep the home together. Some of the wives were given needlework to do at headquarters, but, as an Annual Report so characteristically points out; "They did nothing to foster the notion that the wife and not the husband is the proper person to maintain the household."

The Church Army labour homes became overcrowded, for many men selected from the King's tents were sent to them for more continuous training. This led to the purchase of the Yorkshire Stingo Brewery, 187 Marylebone Road, when it came on to the market in 1909, for use as a new central labour home. Little did the purchasers think that in 1965 the site would become the new headquarters of the Church Army. As a central labour home it was admirable, for it could accommodate not only a labour home with workshop and dormitories, but also a workshop for men found sleeping on the Thames embankment, an additional relief workshop for married men, and a home and workshop for first offenders.

Another way of helping the married man and his family was the city garden scheme which was started in 1909.

There were many vacant plots at that time in the City and nearby, and the Church Army would obtain permission to use them on a temporary basis. They would then be divided into allotments of about one-sixteenth of an acre and handed over to some needy family man to cultivate. He would have to pay an entrance fee of 1s., returnable on leaving, and for the first year plants and seeds, manure and the use of tools would be free. After that, the man was expected to meet his own costs from the sale of his products, and also to provide vegetables and fruits for his family. The scheme was highly successful during the first world war, and continued well into the twenties, only coming to an end as these plots of land began to be needed for building sites.

As is usual in times of heavy unemployment, young lads experienced great difficulty in finding work when they left school. The Boys' Aid Department, also opened in 1909, helped these lads as best they could. A register of those known to the Church Army was kept at headquarters, and they were placed in the care of suitable people in their parishes. Some were apprenticed, others sponsored at some employment agency, and the Church Army tried to house those who had inadequate homes. Up to 1909 the Church Army had only one home for such boys, Walmer House in Notting Hill, but in that year Stanley House at Stonebridge Park was purchased. It had a large garden, and many of the boys could be taught how to grow vegetables, fruit, and flowers. Some would then find jobs as under-gardeners, and many would emigrate.

Between 1910 and 1914, when the emigration of men practically ceased, a very large number of these boys were sent to Canada or Australia. After a short training at Stanley House they would go for a few months to Hempstead Hall to learn the elements of agriculture, the care of cattle and horses, and poultry keeping. They would come to London for a week to be fitted out with clothes and necessary equipment, and to say farewell to their friends

E

and relatives. Then they would sail, in the charge of a Church Army captain, to the colonies, and he would be responsible for seeing that they found suitable jobs, and were well cared for.

During the first world war there was no longer any need for elaborate plans for helping the homeless and destitute. The resources of the Church Army were, therefore, diverted to the requirements of servicemen at home and abroad. When the war came to an end, the immediate problem was the resettlement of families whose menfolk had returned from the forces. Housing was expensive and difficult to find, and many families had to live in very cramped conditions. Therefore some of the Church Army huts, which had been used during the war for servicemen and munition workers, were adapted as social centres, where all the members of the family could find some sort of amusement in the evenings. The red shield, which had become a familiar sign to many thousands of servicemen, was hung over the doorway, and it was hoped that those who had used the Church Army huts during the war would be attracted to them in peacetime.

By the end of the nineteen-twenties there were at least sixty of these social centres, serving as places to which men and women could come to find friends and enjoy communal interests. Though run with the permission of the local vicar, they were not usually attached to the church, so that those who came would not feel that religion was being foisted upon them. The activities which they provided varied widely and depended upon the particular needs of the district where they were situated and the people they served. The large social centre at Combe Down, Bath, resembled a village club, with its tennis courts, its garden where members could sit and where teas were served in the summer, and its indoor games for the winter and wet weather. The centre at East Ham, which catered more for the younger set and the un-attached, had cricket, cycling, football, boxing and other clubs, and a large canteen which served all types of meals. Perhaps the main importance of these centres was the personal influence which the captain and his wife could exert by being on hand to listen to anyone who wanted to talk, and by helping those who were lonely or new to the district to make friends.

Homelessness and destitution were still problems of the period between the two wars though they were a slightly different character than before the first world war. There was less of the appalling poverty, dirt and raggedness which characterized the destitution of the nineteenth century. Instead of the lowness of the wage, it was intermittent employment which was the cause of much of the poverty in the twenties. Many of the men who returned from the forces found it difficult to adjust themselves to peacetime occupations, and the government's deflationary policy, while it kept prices reasonably stable, left many people without employment. Though social insurance, which had been introduced in 1911, covered many workers by the 1920's, some for various reasons were unable to claim it, and others who had been unemployed for long periods found that they had reached the stage when they could no longer draw benefits. Thus, there were many who were hungry and forced to sleep out.

At first the Church Army followed its accustomed policy of labour homes and hostels for men in need, though it now used the term "work-aid" to describe its methods. A Church Army captain, faced with the problems of a destitute man might say to him: "You are homeless and hungry. Well that's enough for tonight. Come off this cold embankment to our receiving home at Westminster; there's a supper and bed for you and welcome. But if you want more you must show that you are willing to work. Here's a little job; will you do it and earn your breakfast?"

As the twenties progressed and distress deepened, the Church Army had to introduce emergency plans once more. Soup and bread canteens were opened at most of its work-aid homes and social centres, where free food was provided in the winter to those who were suitably recommended. Wives and families were served in the mornings, but men had to wait until the afternoons to give them the opportunity of first seeking work. The numbers sleeping out on the Thames embankment rose, and the authorities began to collect these men at their Hungerford Bridge office, and distribute them among the various charitable agencies, of which the Church Army was one. The Church Army, therefore, had these men as well as those who came to them of their own accord, and their homes again began to be overcrowded. The pre-war method of using tents for the overflow was no longer regarded with favour, and so a search began for a building suitable for a large new work-aid home. It was found eventually at 46 Great Peter Street, just behind Westminster Abbey, and opened in October, 1925, as the King George's Embankment Work-Aid Home.

This home contained three types of help, to be given according to the readiness of the man to work. On the ground floor

the cold and hungry man, directed to the Home by the police or some other friendly adviser, finds himself welcomed with a bowl of good soup and bread, hot water for a wash, and a comfortable bed. There is nothing to pay, and no conditions to fulfil; that he is homeless is his one qualification for admission. After his free night's lodging he is offered his breakfast if he is willing to do a little work (wood chopping mostly) to earn it. Breakfast over, he is bound to think, "Well, I'm just where I was yesterday. No work, no home." And so the Officer-in-charge explains the C.A. work-aid principle, and asks him if he really wants to get higher than the ground floor. Yes, he does. Then follows the three days' work test, and if that is passed—it is more a test of willingness than of capacity—the man is admitted as an inmate of the Home. He goes upstairs to another floor—a step nearer to independence. He is no pauper, and he is made to feel that he is not. The rules to be kept are few and simple; chief among them—cleanliness and no drink. Meanwhile the man who had almost forgotten how to work gradually gets back his moral and physical muscle. The top floor at King George's is the "hotel" section. It is let off in cubicles, at a cheap rate, to men who have found jobs outside, but who desire to stay in the Home for reasons of economy or prudence. They enjoy the privileges of the cheap dining-room, refreshment-bar and billiard room downstairs, together with the aristocratic peace and seclusion of their own quarters.

When every bed in the home was full, room was found in the chapel for a few more, for round its walls were lockers which, when needed, could be converted into quite comfortable beds.

Unemployment continued to increase until by 1929 it had reached all groups in the community, from the school leaver to the older man, and from the working to the professional classes. Soon it became impossible even for the ordinary man to find a job, and he might remain without work not merely for several months, but for a year or so. His resources would be completely used up, his family on the point of starvation, and he himself so utterly dejected that he would soon be unable to work.

On the night of October 1, 1929, Church Army officers conducted an extensive survey of the London area to estimate the full extent of this need, and were astounded at the large number of men who were desperately anxious to find work. An annexe to the Embankment Home had already been added in the Waterloo Road where latecomers could be received, and this was now opened earlier in the evening and as many taken in as possible. There was greater pressure on work-aid accommodation and so the premises at the work-aid home in Star Road, West Kensington were extended, and several other work-aid homes enlarged. Figures for December 1929 showed admissions to the Waterloo Road shelter of over 3,000, of which only

700 refused to work for their breakfast. They also showed
that some 450 were under twenty-one years of age.

It was past eleven o'clock at night when I arrived at the
Waterloo Road Shelter for homeless men; and I sat at the
extreme left of the table. It was, therefore, not possible to
see the applicants until, one by one, they were called into
the room. The impression remains a very vivid one. Some of
the men moved smartly through the doorway and stood
there framed against the background of light; some shuffled
in; some were clothed in rags and carried bundles of newspapers—real "old stagers". Others came with alacrity and
were smartly dressed. They spoke in cosmopolitan accents—
the unmistakable "cockney", broad North country, an
occasion "Oxford drawl". It was a long procession and
occasionally someone in the office would ask: "How many
more?" "Thirty more." A little later the same question
would be asked. "Forty-five more." The queue awaiting admission was growing faster than the men could be received.
Long after, when all were admitted and fed, and when all
had gone upstairs to the big sleeping room lighted all night
by dull, red lights, we passed out on the nightly patrol
through the streets to search for those to whom the shelter is
perhaps unknown—the newcomers to town, those spending
their first night out, any who care to accept food and shelter
for the rest of the night.

The situation in the next year or so grew from bad to
worse, and for the first time, in 1932, the Waterloo Road
Shelter had to be kept open all the summer. The social
centres were converted into occupational centres, where
facilities for boot-repairing, mending of clothes and simple
carpentry were available, and sometimes classes in shorthand, first-aid and wood-carving were held to give the
men something to do, while a special work-aid room was
opened at headquarters for professional men who had lost
their jobs.

Many of these men came from the provinces to London
to seek work and their wives and children were left behind
to fend for themselves. These became the care of any

Church Army sisters in the district, who would provide them with cheap bread and soup, and arrange for them to have coal and firewood. They would try to see that only those genuinely in need received these things, and this was by no means easy when the extent of the distress was so great.

By the end of the winter of 1934–35 the situation had begun to improve, and some of the more extreme measures could be removed. But there were still many homeless people who had been unemployed for a long time, and whose character and strength needed building up. Therefore a new system was introduced into the work-aid homes. After reception and a test of not more than three days, the men would be invited to become home employees for four months, during which time they would receive an agreed regular wage, out of which they paid for their own meals and board. They could then get their insurance card stamped and be able to prove to any prospective employer that they were no longer workless or work shirkers.

Wilson Carlile House in Stepney was one of the first to adopt this new method. Originally a clothing factory, it had been acquired in 1935 for use as a home for some three hundred destitute men in the East End. It was the most up to date of the homes, with well-appointed bathrooms, wash-basins and footbaths, and a drying-room for wet clothing as well as deep sinks for the washing of clothes. The poorest of the guests were able to cook or heat up their food in the lodgers' kitchen. Cheap meals—a meat breakfast for $4\frac{1}{2}$d. and dinner for 6d.—were provided in the dining-room, and there was a comfortable sitting-room with armchairs, periodicals, a piano, and a billiard table. Upstairs were dormitories with rows of neat beds, the sheets and grey blankets covered with gay pink counterpanes, each bed having a locker seat. On the second floor were cubicles for 1s. a night which contained a bed, a chair and a metal locker. Downstairs there was a work-aid room where professional men were employed in addressing envelopes and delivering circulars and advertisements, and a bakery where men were apprenticed and baked the bread required for the Church Army homes in London.

One of the most urgent problems of the mid-thirties was that of the lad who had left school and was unable to find a job. Since the 1920's, lads coming to seek work in London had been offered a home at Clifton House or in one of the men's hostels until employment could be found for them. But by the 1930's these lads were coming to London in much larger numbers and finding it almost impossible to get work. They soon became disillusioned and joined the ranks of those who were homeless and had to sleep out.

In order to try and prevent this, the Church Army began in 1934 to open a ring of wayside lodges on the outskirts of London, where such lads could stay. They were situated at strategic points, on the Uxbridge Road to attract those coming from Wales and the west of England, at Finchley for those from the depressed areas of the north, on the Brixton Road for those from Southampton and the south coast, and in Stepney for lads from the eastern counties.

Special introduction tickets were given to the police, clergy and other interested people, and anyone coming into contact with such a lad was asked to direct him to one of these lodges, where he could spend the night. The Church Army captain in charge would then get to know him, and either send him to the employers' bureau at headquarters, or find some local work for him to do. Headquarters had for some time kept a list of likely employers, and if the lad could not live in a Church Army hostel the vicar of his London parish was asked to get into touch with him and see that he had suitable lodgings. Many of these lads were sent to train as chefs and caterers in the bakery at Wilson Carlile House in Stepney, and for a time they had their own special accommodation there, which included a dormitory, a recreation-room and their own staircase from the street.

The following is a description of the change which took place in one of these lads:

He stood at the door of Wilson Carlile House, Stepney—a picture of utter despair and hopelessness. His hair untouched by a barber for months, hung in a fringe round the collar of a ragged jacket. There was an accumulation of dirt on his face and neck, and his whole appearance was that of starved and neglected boyhood. He was only seventeen, with a decent education and able to do typing and shorthand efficiently. But unhappy home-life had caused him to "take the road" from the north of England, penniless and friendless. "Jumping a lorry" here for a few miles, tramping and begging, sleeping out and dodging the police, he came in to London from the east side and was directed, almost by chance, to the Church Army Hostel. Two months later the same youth—smart, cheerful and ambitious, but still at the Hostel—looks forward with confidence to a future of useful service to others. In the Hostel kitchen he has been taught by a cook and baker, who have already guided scores of similar youngsters away from wastrelism into skilled craftsmanship, to make good bread, appetizing cakes and pastry, and prepare satisfying meals for two or three hundred hungry men.

These lads were very dear to the heart of Wilson Carlile, so he asked that any gifts for his ninetieth and ninety-first birthdays should be devoted to building a new and up-to-date home for them. The result was the opening of Livingstone House, Stonebridge Park, Willesden, in November 1938, with beds and living space for ninety-one lads, room to play games, to read in quiet, and plenty of hot water for washing and baths. Most of them were lads who had been received at one or other of the wayside lodges and needed more care and help than was available there. Sometimes work was found for them in the district, which at that time had many small industries, or they might commute daily into a job in central London. They would make Livingstone House their home for a while, and even when they gave up living there they were encouraged to return when unemployed or in any need.

The second world war, like the first, led to the employment of most people. The Church Army homes and hostels were again used for the forces, for those employed in government factories, and for others who had to work in places away from their homes. When the war ended there was a similar problem of adjustment to civilian life. For a time, headquarters was engaged in trying to find jobs for the demobbed, and the hostels in London and the provinces were in great demand for those on their way home or trying to find employment.

But with more than enough jobs available, the problems of the homeless man in the late forties were very different from what they had been in the twenties and thirties. Such a man usually had been involved in difficulties at home or at work and decided to get away from them. Finding himself in a strange town he might be tempted into bad company and join the ever-increasing band of criminals and black marketeers. If he could be helped over this bad patch in a human and friendly way he might be restored to his previous life, or at least helped to make a new one. King George's Embankment Home was handed back to the Church Army in 1945, and was reopened as King George's Hostel for the reception and help of men found homeless in central London, and in 1947 the Nelson Square Church Army Centre was started for the homeless men of the embankment.

The growth of the welfare state meant yet another process of adaptation for the Church Army. Social insurance and social assistance, which now included everyone, ensured a minimum standard of living for all. It therefore seemed as if this aspect of Church Army work was a thing of the past. But this was not so, and the Annual Report for 1949–50 explains that "the welfare state is not complete in itself. The opportunities for sympathetic advice, a place to lay one's head, a helping hand into a job, the means of re-uniting man and wife" are still needed.

The welfare hostel has now become the centre of men's social work. Some, which had been labour homes, were rebuilt, and others completely refurnished to bring them into line with similar accommodation. Dormitories were converted into individual cubicles and tastefully decorated. More baths and wash-basins were added, the dining-room provided with individual tables, and the sitting-room with easy chairs, a wireless, and later a television.

The main purpose of these hostels is to provide cheap and comfortable accommodation for working men, especially those who have to live away from home for a time. The age range is very wide. Youngsters coming into town for their first job may begin by living there. Old-age pensioners are always welcome, and usually some special accommodation is reserved for them so that they may be together, and have somewhere to stay in the daytime. There are men out of prison, whose past is known only to the warden, men on probation, and ex-patients from mental hospitals. Much of the work in the hostels is done by those who are slightly handicapped or have had some illness which prevents them from finding full employment.

As you walk about London, you will sometimes see *Church Army Men's Hostel* written on the walls of some of the big Victorian houses that give such spacious accommodation. In the daytime, you will see little sign of life. The large, quiet rooms are empty; but in the Captain's office all is busy. Accommodation plans have to be changed to meet day-to-day needs, newcomers have to be fitted out with clothes sometimes, and there are always employment problems calling for help and advice. Night after night, new men arrive; each with their own particular problem, each with a desperate need for care and kindness. To quote the words of one of the Captains-in-Charge, these temporary homes are *stepping stones* to something better; they help men who have lost their courage to "find their feet" and get good jobs again. Men who have had disappointment and illness can come to these hostels (at very small cost) and build up their strength. Here, in the quiet atmosphere of the house, where spiritual help soon brings a new contentment, they regain their hold on life. In a short time, they are well enough to get back into the rough and tumble of everyday life and find their own way.

Today there are five of these hostels in London, and eighteen of them in provincial cities.

One of the London hostels is for professional men, who for one reason or another are without employment or anywhere to live. Some are from prison, others from mental hospitals, but many have some deep personal reason which has made them unable to carry on. These men had come to the notice of Wilson Carlile in the early twenties, and special clerical work had been given to them at the Central Labour Home in the Marylebone Road, and this work was particularly needed at a time when such men were not covered by social insurance. Prebendary Treacher took a personal interest in them and continued to help them even after he had to resign from full-time work with the Church Army. Then it became obvious that a special Church Army hostel was needed, designed to give these men a background that would help them in their difficulties. An ordinary house in a northern suburb was found, and opened in 1948 as a guest house for them. A report gives some idea of this work.

Most men who seek our help have arrived at the brink of a chasm. Behind them is the position they formerly held in society. In front of them, on the other side of the chasm, is the unknown future, and it is our privilege to assist them in filling that chasm and to guide them into an establishment of their future. The work involved is not simply the provision of board and lodging; that is, of course a first essential; but it is the beginning only. There is the necessity of a period of readjustment, prior to seeking and taking up employment. In order to allow for this we employ men at our Headquarters, paying them a modest wage which allows them to pay for their upkeep and necessary expenses. After a while, when we think a man is prepared, mentally and physically to seek permanent employment, we discuss the prospects and do our utmost to establish him.

Church Army work for homeless men has therefore changed greatly in character throughout the years, partly because the needs have changed, and partly because the State has taken over increasing responsibility for it. Today the Church Army is largely involved in helping men who, for one reason or another, do not fit into the State scheme, and who need more personal care than either the State or other voluntary societies can provide.

UNATTACHED WOMEN AND GIRLS

Women with no money and no home will usually try to find somewhere to live, even if it is the smallest and most poverty-stricken hovel. This was why only about ten per cent of the homeless and destitute who asked for shelter at the end of the nineteenth century were women. But many of these women had to resort to prostitution in order to keep their independence, and so the Church Army sisters were willing, from the first, to give any homeless woman a shelter for the night, and then try to find work and more suitable accommodation for her. Social work for women became a very important part of the life of the Church Army sister, and it included helping those who were on the verge of destitution, as well as those who had already become homeless or were earning their living on the streets.

At first, destitute women who came to the Church Army were treated in a similar manner to men, and a labour home was opened for them at 238 Marylebone Road in 1891. They were given laundry work to do and after six months they were placed in employment. The Women's Help Department was responsible for this, and opened several other labour homes for women. But this method of helping destitute women was not nearly so successful as it

was with men, for on the whole the women did not like the
confinement and the discipline involved. Therefore, in a
very short time, the Church Army closed its labour homes
for women and tried to deal with them in other ways.

Those who were desperately in need of work were employed in the workroom at headquarters, usually on sewing, and were paid from the proceeds of the articles which
they made. Others were found jobs as domestic servants,
or in any occupation with which they were familiar. The
Women's Help Department continued for years to provide
work for women who were temporarily destitute, and to
find employment of a more permanent nature for the
others.

These women would often have to live in one of the
common lodging houses, where they would mix with
habitual criminals and confirmed prostitutes, and where
there was great overcrowding and little opportunity for
personal cleanliness or for maintaining the decencies of
life. Therefore the sisters were overjoyed when, as an experiment, the London County Council asked the Church
Army to take over the supervision of one of these lodging
houses and provide a decent home for its inmates. The
choice fell upon a common lodging house in Great Peter
Street, almost beneath the shadow of Westminster Abbey
and yet in one of the most unsalubrious districts of London.
This was acquired in 1913; the sisters moved in and
gradually introduced more cleanliness and respectable
living. Many of the old lodgers stayed, and came to appreciate the greater comfort. Among the regulars were several
elderly people who had made this place their home for as
long as fifteen years, managing to pay the small fee by
selling matches and other wares in the street. Most of the
girls and younger women were flower sellers, supplement-
ing their income by prostitution, and a few of the middle-
aged did sewing. In line with the other common lodging
houses, the sister-in-charge asked no questions as to the
character or occupation of those who applied, but just

made friends with them. In time confidences might be exchanged, and some of the women would eventually move to other Church Army homes, or manage to earn enough to rent a room of their own.

Peter House was pulled down in 1934, but not before Queen Mary Hostel in Greencoat Place replaced it. This was a more modern building and, when its extensions were completed, could take many more residents. There were cubicles as well as dormitories, and a canteen serving lunch and tea for any who were not at work.

A woman will arrive in the hall, probably only carrying a carrier-bag and maybe that's all she possesses at that time. She has wandered about from place to place trying to find accommodation and having very little money or maybe none at all and at last the police have said: "Try the Church Army!" and she comes to us almost losing hope, and we say, "Hello!" and she will say: "Can you take me in?" and then often seeing how hungry she must be by the look of her, how tired she must be and, worse still, how hopeless . . . she is welcomed in and given food, a bed, a towel, soap, encouraged to have a bath and then to bed. That's not the end, of course. In the morning we ask her what she intends to do and often the answer is: "I want a job." She may stay at the hostel for a time, and then when her earnings permit, find more suitable accommodation.

The doors of Queen Mary Hostel are still open to those who can afford very little, who are not strong enough to make much of life, or have nowhere else to live. Some work in the catering trade and have very varied hours. Others are employed in office cleaning and start early in the morning. Some are mentally or physically incapable of earning much but want to keep their independence. These will probably stay until they die. The hostel becomes their home and they can spend the whole day there, buying their meals at the canteen. A little courtyard, once the entrance to the stables, has been converted into a garden, and here, in the middle of London, they can sit and enjoy the sunshine whenever the weather permits.

Portman House, Marylebone, which was a similar hostel, was acquired from the Shaftesbury Society in 1933. The people who lived there were largely working women who used it as a place to go to between jobs, or when pulling themselves together after some mishap, casuals who came for the night or two, and old-age pensioners, who made the place their permanent home. Portman House had to be closed in 1953, and was replaced by Elgood House, Marylebone, which can accommodate some hundred women. Like Queen Mary Hostel, it has a beautiful chapel, furnished with fabrics supplied and paid for by the residents.

Since hostels such as these expect some payment, however small, there has always been the need for an emergency hostel to take the penniless, stranded woman. Several homes have served this purpose at different times. Before the first world war, the East London home, opened near Victoria Park in 1903, took in the older homeless and destitute woman, and a home near Shepherd's Bush helped the younger woman who had come to London to seek employment. After the war, Queen Lodge, off the Edgware Road, was opened for young girls who were stranded, most of them having run away from home and been picked up by the police or found wandering round Paddington Station. Belvedere Crescent, near Waterloo, was for the older woman who had nowhere else to go, and it combined an emergency shelter with a working women's hostel, so that when a woman had found work she could continue living in the building.

The unemployment of the late twenties made the need for a larger emergency hostel more urgent, so the Women's Embankment Home, in Boniface Street, Westminster, was opened. A soup supper, with a bath and bed, was provided, and there was tea and bread and butter for breakfast. In the morning friendly inquiries would be made with regard to their future plans, and, if they had none, temporary work in the home or a visit to headquarters would be suggested. When it was found necessary to provide more accommodation the White Hart, near Westminster, was acquired, and opened by the Queen in 1935. The bars and taproom were transformed into a living-room and dormitory, with bathrooms and further sleeping accommodation upstairs. Fifty homeless women and girls could spend the night there, and, as in the men's hostels at that time, extra pull-down beds were available in the chapel to meet an excess demand.

Since then, the emergency hostel for women has changed its location several times. It was in Bryanston Street during and after the second world war, then near Victoria, and it now occupies the old training college building in Cosway Street, which has been adapted to take ninety women. Its first two customers were a blind woman who was in London for a braille test, and a woman seeking hospital treatment. There are many types of people in the emergency hostel.

> They include women of low mentality who cannot cope with life; those changing jobs; those attending hospital who are unable to work; those discharged from hospital who have no work; West Indians who have not been met; people who have been evicted.

People on probation, discharged prisoners, alcoholics and many others in distress find their way there. Since national assistance is now available for all, a small charge is made for board and lodging, but this is not asked for until the morning, and the door is opened at all times of the night for the genuinely homeless person.

Among the homeless and destitute, there have always been women accustomed to a better standard of living, and this was particularly the case in the late Victorian era, when unmarried women and widows were not trained to earn their living. Gentlewomen in need have for a long time been a concern of the Church Army. The Private

F

Aid Department was started at the beginning of the century to help them in a variety of ways. It was customary at that time for the middle-class family to look after any of its members in distress, but sometimes they could not, or they would not, and then the person was left to fend for herself. The chief jobs available for "ladies" were as governesses, companions, or skilled needlewomen, and they were difficult to get, and rarely permanent, especially as the person grew older.

The Private Aid Department might find such a person work or provide her with some work at headquarters, it might put her into touch with some other agency which could help, or it might give her clothing, food or fuel, and sometimes a small sum of money to tide over an emergency. But monetary aid was usually given from funds earmarked for the purpose, rather than from those of the Society.

Today the Private Aid Department has become the Distressed Gentlewomen's Department, and the people who seek its help are usually elderly and have seen better times. Many have suffered some tragedy which has made life close in upon them.

> You are over seventy years of age. When your husband deserted you, you were already in the late fifties. After the first shock and heartbreak, you pulled yourself together and opened a small restaurant. This you managed very well until recently, when you received another shock. The premises were sold on which you ran your little business, and you lost the chance of continuing to earn your living. . . .

> You are a widow in the seventies. You have the ever-present agonies of a precious only son who is mentally sick, and your beloved only daughter, cruelly deserted by her husband, now a helpless invalid. Both will always need to be looked after, and there is no-one but you to do it.

These are typical of the cases with which the Department deals today.

After the second world war the Church Army, for a

time, helped some families which had been evicted from their lodgings and were awaiting the allocation of a council house. Their hostels were not equipped to take mothers with young children, and therefore in 1953 Stanley House, Willesden, was adapted for the purpose. In line with the statutory regulations for local authorities, only mothers and children were accepted, and the fathers had to find their own lodgings, though the Church Army welfare hostels were always available for them.

"They seem to spend quite a pleasant, normal day here," says the sister-in-charge. "In the morning there is housework, in the afternoon the mothers take their children out, weather permitting, and in the evening they sit in the big rest room and chat, knit or sew, watch TV (which they hire and pay for between themselves) and have their husbands and other visitors in. Or they can go out, knowing that there are plenty of people about the house to give an eye to the little ones."

Another group of women for whom the Church Army has always shown great concern are the promiscuous, and ways of helping them have changed with the times. In the late nineteenth century many homeless women were obliged to earn their living, at least temporarily, as prostitutes, for it was difficult to find suitable and permanent employment. A prison chaplain, writing at that time, estimated that about half the prostitutes sentenced were domestic servants, and one-tenth had been laundresses, charwomen, factory hands and seamstresses, all occupations subject to irregular employment.

It was easy for a girl at the end of her tether to make money in this way. Certain streets in the big cities were known to be frequented by prostitutes. Thus, when the Church Army mission-nurses were first recruited, the Report for 1887 says: "Certain nights are partly spent in seeking and rescuing the fallen, mostly being at or near Charing Cross." The next year a mission-nurse was appointed by the Bishop of Southwell "to visit the sick and suffering at the fairs, and to carry on rescue work among the gipsies". This form of social work was one of the duties of the mission sister from the very beginning of the Church Army, even before her brother officer had become involved in work other than pure evangelism.

It was always desirable to get into touch with these girls before prostitution had become a habit, and so in 1889 Church Army mission nurses started to "scour the streets round Edgware Road and Lisson Grove at midnight, to hold meetings and approach individuals, some of whom they found came from respectable homes and had been led away by false promises, others had left home to find employment and pleasure, while many were inured to this sort of life". Two sisters would usually go out at night, together, into the streets with bunches of flowers or copies of the *Church Army Gazette* to which a card, inviting the girl to come to the shelter for a cup of tea, was attached. At first they probably took those girls who were willing into their own home, until they could find a society which would care for them more permanently. But there is mention of a temporary shelter in London during the winters of 1891 and 1892.

More permanent shelters were opened at Nutford Place and Hendon in 1895 and 1896 and also in many provincial towns, where they were known as "rescue stations". These shelters were ordinary small houses with seven or eight rooms, and no indication as to their function. The girls would stay there until other arrangements could be made for them, and they would help the sisters with their housework and cooking, while the sisters, in their turn, would be getting to know them better. Some of the girls could be sent home, employment would be found for others, but a few would have to go to another home for training before they were suitable for ordinary work.

The rescue home in Stourcliffe Street, Marylebone, which was opened in 1900, was for many years the centre for this work, and the home where the sisters received their practical training.

> The work carried on at Stourcliffe Street comprises midnight rescue work, midnight meetings (weekly in winter), systematic visiting of low lodging houses in search of young girls, services in casual wards, visiting girls in hospitals and workhouses, and in their own lodgings. Flats of doubtful character receive much attention, our workers visiting from door to door, with parish notices supplied by the clergy, and judiciously leaving our address with offers of help when a suitable opening occurs. Hyde Park is also frequently visited at a late hour, when numbers of women, some of them quite young, receive offers of shelter and protection through our workers.

Moral welfare thus became an important aspect of the work of the Church Army sister, and it was carried on according to the established methods of that time. Girls were sought for in the streets at night, sheltered until a suitable permanent home could be found for them, and then sent to this home for, what we would call today, rehabilitation.

For some time the Church Army had no permanent, or long-stay, homes of its own, and had to use those of the Church Penitentiary Association or the Reformatory and Refuge Union. Then, in 1908, the management of St. Helena's at Margate was handed over to the Church Army. But the most important acquisition was that of the Albion Hill Homes at Brighton, which were taken over from Mrs. Vicars in 1916. She had been one of the outstanding pioneers in moral welfare work and had insisted upon specialized homes for different types of girls. The Brighton Homes consisted of four houses, each with its own facilities, so that the houses could be used for entirely different purposes. One became a long-stay home, the second a home for unmarried mothers where they could have their babies and live there with them for several months, the third was a home for the treatment of

venereal disease, and the fourth a small home for alcoholics and drug addicts. Thus it became possible, within a
small community, to help many different types of girls.

The first world war, with the greater emancipation of
women and other social changes, introduced a different
approach to this form of welfare work. For one thing,
much of the Victorian reticence was gone, and the subject
could be discussed more openly and objectively. Rescue
and reform still remained the principles on which such
work was carried out, and the girls washed, scrubbed and
polished to restore their virtue. But it began to be realized
that, though the problem was basically a moral one, many
other causative factors were present. This made it necessary to revise the training of the sisters engaged in the
work, and in 1924 a special course of theoretical and practical training was introduced, to be taken after the general
course at the training college. The sisters were made
familiar with conditions at police courts, workhouses and
lodging houses, they undertook night work under supervision, and helped with an experienced worker in some of
the homes. This was in line with the developments in
training which were taking place elsewhere, for in 1920
the Josephine Butler Memorial House had been opened in
Liverpool and undertook most of the training of moral
welfare workers.

For some time the Church Army trained its own workers
at the centre in Paddington, which offered good opportunities for practical work. But in 1948 three sisters took
the year's course at Josephine Butler Memorial House, and
others attended the shorter London course. The courses at
Josephine Butler College have now become the normal way
for equipping the sisters with the specialized knowledge
which they need, and a Church Army sister is now the
principal of the College.

Meanwhile, diocesan moral welfare had become more
fully organized. The Church of England Advisory Board
for Moral Welfare Work had been set up in 1932 with

organizing secretaries in all the dioceses. Church Army sisters began to work more closely with the diocesan moral welfare associations and often under the direction of the local committee. In fact, by 1957 two sisters were themselves organizing secretaries, and this link with the work in the dioceses has continued. The sisters also co-operate with other agencies doing similar work, and attend conferences connected with such work. This is in accord with present-day tendencies which draw social workers more closely together.

The first world war also introduced changes in the types of homes which were available. Before this the girl had usually gone to the workhouse to have her baby, and left the child there when she was well enough to seek work, so that if she eventually agreed to enter a rescue home the child offered no problem. The Church Army was not very happy about this, and in 1914 St. Ann's Home in Wandsworth was converted into a mother-and-baby home, which accepted mothers with their first babies after leaving hospital, and kept them for a year while the mother was training for domestic service. A difficulty then arose if the mother could not take the child with her to a job, and so the Babies' Boarding Home at Turner House, near Regent's Park, was opened to care for the children while the mothers went out to work. Each mother was expected to contribute towards the cost and to visit whenever possible. Thus, the emphasis was moving away from what the girl had done to the future needs of the girl herself and her baby.

Another advance made in the inter-war period was the use of specialized homes for certain types of girls. In 1919 St. Monica's at Croydon was opened for young girls who had suffered from indecent assault, or lived in immoral surroundings. It was a beautiful house, with lawns and gardens, and the girls lived and were educated there. Domestic training, cooking and household duties, laundry, gardening and poultry keeping were taught, as well as the usual school lessons, and each girl was allowed to choose what she wanted to do. Then, when she was old enough to work, the Church Army employment bureau at headquarters found her a job.

Crathorne House, at Finchley, which was opened in 1920, was intended for girls whose mentality was slightly below the normal. The girl could keep her baby with her until the age of six or seven, when the child was sent to a children's home. The mother might eventually have to go to a home for the subnormal, but quite often she improved so much with care and understanding that it was possible to place her in a suitable job.

The Church Army was also concerned for girls who were wild and undisciplined, who refused to live at home, and who had undesirable friends and acquaintances. The Frances Owen Home was handed over to the Church Army in 1900 for such girls, and for a short time St. Ann's Home in Wandsworth was used for the purpose. Sometimes the girl would come of her own accord, but more often she was sent by the authorities because her parents had found her unmanageable or the police had discovered her roaming the streets.

> The purpose of the home is to save the girls, and to this end a code of rules and discipline is instituted; system runs through the whole gamut of work; provision is made for giving the girls plenty of healthy recreation; the food is abundant and varied; the life of the Home is so regulated that the girls are face to face all the time with object lessons of just what is essential to a good and useful life, and the spirit of a happy and simple religion diffuses everything. But the secret charm is not in any of these methods or in all combined. The supreme recreating force is, after all, very human, when the discovery is made that the sister cares for them.

This is what a Church Army preventive home was like before the first world war.

After the war there were the two large "training"

homes, as they became called. One was Trewint at Bexley Heath which had been taken over by the Church Army in 1916. This was for schoolgirls, many of whom were sent to the Home by the Poor Law guardians. They lived at Trewint for one or two years and were trained for domestic service. Holly Bush Lodge, Southgate, took a slightly older and more educated type of girl, though one quite uncontrolled and undisciplined. Laundry and needlework were taught as well as domestic work, so that the girl, if she wanted, could take a job other than that of domestic service.

The training homes today at St. Leonards and Derby are very different. The girls still come from difficult homes where their parents are unable or unwilling to care for them properly. But there is much more freedom. The girls do much of the housework, so that they will know how to manage their own homes when they marry. But most of them, after the first few months, go out to local jobs, either part-time or full-time, in shops or factories, so that the sister-in-charge has an opportunity of helping them to adjust to regular work. They mingle freely with other girls in the neighbourhood, attend the parish church and go to local clubs, and they no longer go around in caps and aprons, to differentiate them from other people.

Similarly, moral welfare work itself has undergone a great change. Few of the girls today who come to the sisters for help can be described as prostitutes, for few of them are intent upon earning a living in this way. The days of the friendless, betrayed or destitute girl who had to take to the streets are past. Instead, the girls who need help are usually expectant mothers who are unmarried, and who come to the sister of their own accord or on the recommendation of some social worker, doctor, friend or clergyman. They are mostly young people who have been experimenting with sex, and are surprised, upset or annoyed at what has happened, and whose parents are unwilling to stand by them. They need somewhere to go while waiting for their baby and some help to settle down afterwards into ordinary life. The Church Army has two homes for unmarried mothers, the Limes which cares for the older girl both before and after her confinement, and St. Christopher's which has recently been converted into a home for schoolgirl mothers, with arrangements with the local authorities to carry on their education.

An experiment which the Church Army is in the process of making is to help the father of the child as well as the unmarried mother. For as Josephine Butler never ceased to point out, it is the man who is as much responsible for the situation as the woman. For a year or so now a Church Army captain has been working among unmarried fathers in the Chichester diocese, and another captain has been appointed to the Chelmsford diocese. Their work brings them into close touch with many family problems as they are envisaged by the man, and also with those of the homo-sexual.

The sisters, too, are broadening the scope of their work, and taking an interest in other members of the family as well as in the girl who comes to them for help. They try to become a family friend, and in doing so may be able to prevent some family problems arising, and to deal with others at an early stage before they reach a crisis. They also take part in youth activities, and may be members of the local youth council, so that they have an opportunity of imparting an understanding of sex, marriage, and family life to the young people.

Excessive drinking is another problem with which the sisters have frequently had to deal. Temperance work, as it was called in the early days, was the special concern of Miss Gay, and she was largely responsible for the opening of the inebriates' home at Eltham at the beginning of the century, and of the new home at Isleworth in 1908. Women were received from all classes of the community, although the home at Eltham eventually became a home for those of the middle class. Some were sent by the poor law guardians, a few came from the courts, but many came of their own accord, on the advice of Church Army officers, or perhaps a clergyman or social worker. They followed the old-fashioned cure of frequent meals and special lozenges to affect their taste, and were kept busy all day long with gardening, needlework, or laundrywork.

Bethany is the successor of these homes for inebriates, and here the drink and drug addict, the woman contemplating suicide, or those in any sort of trouble, will find a friend and help. It was in 1936 that one of the sisters went with a news team to Hyde Park and was astounded at the number of drunken women and girls who tried to hinder the meeting.

"I would like to do something for these girls," she told the Chief, "if I could have a little room," and she was given what she asked for in Portman House. This room gradually became a sort of informal club for those who were determined to try to fight drink or some other obsession. It has moved its location several times, but the women who need help know where to find it, and usually manage to turn up when they are desperate. Help is given through friendliness, so that visiting the Bethany sister becomes a habit.

It was hard work at first, while the tradition was being established, for the drunkards were often so drunk that they spoiled the place for the others, but they eventually came to realize that the peace of Bethany was too valuable to be spoiled. A club night, a cup of tea, and a conversation with the sister, are the treatment which Bethany offers, and it is the knowledge that she can come at any time of the day or night to Bethany which often keeps a woman straight. Many, of course, are never cured, but some are, and owe a new lease of life to the Bethany sister and the God to whom she introduces them.

Thus, in essentials, the work that the Church Army is doing today for women and girls is not very different from what it has always tried to do. It is meeting these people at the point of their need and doing its best to help them with their problems. But the methods which are followed have changed greatly with the years, as a deepening understanding has developed with regard to the problems themselves. It is realized that anti-social behaviour is often caused by some psychological reason, and the Church Army, through its newly formed counselling centre, is now able to help in this respect.

ORDINARY FAMILIES

Even the family of the ordinary working man often needed help at the time when the Church Army was first formed. For although skilled workmen could generally find reasonably permanent employment, the unskilled might have a succession of jobs with long intervals between them. The family income at the best of times did little more than cover the cost of food and rent, with scarcely anything over for clothes or any other expense. In the less good periods food was scarce, possessions were pawned, and the standard of living fell to a very low level.

The "Old Clo" department of the Church Army was a great boon to such families. Started as the Church Army Salesroom in 1889, it occupied a room behind the evangelists' training home and sold clothing, shoes, furniture and crockery at nominal prices to those recommended by the sisters and captains. Many a poor family was enabled to set up house again, and the children provided with warm clothes and boots which they had probably never had before. Later "Old Clo" was to be found in the basement of headquarters, where "twice a day came the poorest of the mothers of poverty stricken London to buy clothes at nominal prices, as their scanty means permitted. From Willesden, Stepney, Vauxhall, Kilburn and Battersea they came—these women who all clutched a precious ticket given to them by a clergyman or district visitor." This was the "Old Clo" department as it was in 1914. In later years it moved to Shillibeer Place where it continued its much needed service.

"Even today", says a Church Army captain, "with a Welfare State, we find a real need for the continuance of this special work which is truly in the old Church Army tradition."

Social insurance and assistance help many people, but those who qualify for this often find that they have little to spare for things other than their daily needs. There are also many elderly folk who do not qualify for a pension at the full rate, and people who are hit by sudden disaster. Immediate help can be given from the Clothing Department, which is now housed in a building in the grounds of Livingstone House, Willesden.

Families were also helped in the past by the Sunbeam Mission, which was one of several organizations formed to create a better understanding between working and middle-class people. It was started in 1891 as an independent mission, and handed over to the Church Army after the first world war. Its beginning is typical of the period.

The Sunbeam Mission originated from a small private Bible Class held in the drawing-room of the late Mrs. Battiscombe of Weston-super-Mare, for her own and her friends' children. She realized they had no idea and could form no opinion of the conditions under which very poor children lived, and she thought a good way of enlightening them would be for each child to undertake to befriend a poor child, and do all they could to brighten their lives.

"Sunbeams" were quickly enrolled, each was placed in touch with a child in a poor family and was expected to send a magazine once a month to the child, and if possible write at Christmas and birthdays. Often the contact with the child led to friendship with the whole family. Help would be given in illness, holidays arranged, and the poorer family would feel that it could appeal to its "sunbeam" family in any particular need. "Sunbeams" were especially helpful at the time of the depression in the early thirties, and in some cases they took their poorer friends into their own homes during the second world war.

When there was little money in a household, it was not only possessions which were lacking. Health suffered too, for, in the days before the health service, medicines had to be purchased, doctors paid for, and there was rarely anything left for a holiday or a rest from work. If a mother or her children were ill there was no one from whom to seek advice, and neighbours had to be relied upon in child-birth. It is little wonder, therefore, that the first Church Army sisters were called mission-nurses, and spent much of their time in nursing those they visited. When the mission-nurse was first commissioned it was intended that

> she should be a bona fide nurse, with enough experience to make her, when on duty in a parish, an almost indispensable person. She was not a trained nurse, but she did attend courses of nursing lectures, had slight experience in a London infirmary, and a certificate of first aid. This made her able to deal with the simple illnesses and accidents of the home, and to bring comfort to those who were lying ill in their beds.

Even when, in 1906, her name was changed to mission-sister, much of her work was still caring for those who were ill, though by this time district nurses were more numerous and relieved her of the more serious cases. Yet many women were still unable to obtain the services of a midwife, and this resulted in several Church Army sisters training in midwifery and obtaining the certificate of the Central Midwives Board, which they continued to do until the first world war.

A medical mission for women and children existed for many years in the training home mission hall in Crawford Street, and was used, not only for the medical care of out-patients, but also to give practical experience to mission-nurses in training. Like all the home medical missions of that time, it was needed by families who were too poor to pay for a doctor and found it difficult to get good or quick medical help from the poor law doctor or the hospital clinics. Following the usual custom, a religious service was held while the people were waiting, and tea provided after they had seen the doctor and while their prescriptions were being made up.

The patients would arrive one by one. There were mothers of all ages, from those with new babies, who looked scarcely more than children themselves, to the old women of seventy. Here and there a girl sat among them. Here and there were toddlers and larger lads and lassies; to say nothing of a plentiful sprinkling of babies. Such tidily dressed mothers they were! It would be only a close study of their faces, or by feeling your way sympathetically into their confidence that you could learn how pinched, and straightened, and ground down by poverty they were. Presently a fidgetty youngster in the background heaved a prodigious sigh. And then somebody opened that mysterious cupboard, and down from its top shelf came picture books for some of the little ones. It was not long before the pleasant-faced, kindly doctor turned up; and the patients now began to go upstairs in regular order, moving along the chairs as they emptied.

The Church Army mission-nurses and sisters also visited the patients in their homes and kept in touch with headquarters for anything they might need; and when the doctor ordered a change of surroundings the Fresh Air Fund, which had been started only a little later than the medical mission, made it possible for patients to get a holiday in the country or at the seaside. These benefits were not entirely free. Sixpence was charged for a first visit to the medical mission, and threepence thereafter, and contributions had to be paid into the Fresh Air Fund before a holiday could be taken. But in urgent need, or when the patient was too poor, help was usually forthcoming.

An offshoot of the medical mission was the sanatorium for children at Cookham, Hants. Many of the children brought by their mothers for medical treatment were con-

sumptive and it was almost impossible to find a sanatorium which would take them. The Church Army, therefore, opened its own sanatorium to take children in the
early stages of the illness. According to the methods of
treatment at that time, when they first arrived they were
kept in bed, but as they gained strength they were allowed
up to play with the others. Some went home after about
three months, but others were kept for as long as a year
and a half. After the first world war, when the sanatorium
was moved to Heath End, Farnham, it was confined to
boys, most of whom were sent from the densely populated
areas by the local authorities.

The type of work at the medical mission changed with
developments in medicine. Sun-ray treatment was introduced for children in the nineteen-twenties, and chiropody
for the elderly people in the early nineteen-thirties. Ante-
natal and post-natal clinics were held weekly, where
mothers were taught how to care for their children and
encouraged to bring them regularly, whether or not they
thought they were ill. Similarly, part of the Church Army
housing plan was to provide a few houses with special
veranda accommodation, so that consumptives could be
treated at home. With the introduction of the National
Health Service in 1946 the medical work of the Church
Army was no longer necessary and the medical mission,
which had first opened in 1896, closed its doors for good.

But this was not the case with the holiday homes. These
had been started in 1897 when six cottages were rented at
Great Missenden for mothers with their children to spend
a few days. Then, in 1900, the first Fresh Air Home was
opened at St. Leonards to give mothers with their children
a week by the seaside. A second home at Old Windsor was
lent by Lady Murray for several years for mothers who
needed a quiet rest, and on her death in 1907 this was replaced by a permanent home at Godstone. The Bexhill
Home was acquired in 1906, and this with the St. Leonards Home were the two main holiday homes of the

medical mission for many years, though as the Annual Report for 1906 so truly says:

> We wish we had more of such homes, for there is probably no agency where so much good can be done at so little cost.

Many of those who came to these homes in the early days were sent from the medical mission, and they were often not so much ill as exhausted and depressed. They usually came from the worst of the slums, where a family of eight or nine shared one room, with no facilities to dry the washing, to cook, or even to keep themselves properly clean. The mother might have to supplement the family means by doing some sort of piece-work in the room, and if she were a widow or deserted by her husband, this might be her only source of income. Most of them had not had a holiday before, and some had never seen the sea, so that a fortnight at Bexhill or St. Leonards was a constant source of wonder and amazement.

During the first world war the homes were used for widows or wives of servicemen who were in particular trouble or distress, and when war ended it seemed appropriate to separate the work of the fresh air homes from that of the medical mission, and to make them holiday homes for any families whom the Church Army officers or others recommended. Unemployment was now the main trouble, families often having to live for a long time on a minute income, and this showed itself in overstrain and malnutrition. There were long waiting lists of those who needed a holiday, and a choice had to be made from the families most in need.

The location of the homes changed several times during this inter-war period. A new home was opened at St. Leonards for the poorest mothers and children who were the victims of unemployment and shortage of housing. A house at Salcombe and a bungalow in the New Forest were lent for a season, and in 1924 a children's holiday home was opened at Fleet, in Hampshire. 1933 saw the

G

opening of a holiday home for the people of the north at Southport, in Lancashire, and in 1935 a new home at Weston-super-Mare was opened for mothers and children from South Wales and the Midlands.

A typical day would start with breakfast and family prayers. Mothers and children would then go off to the beach, the children to play or paddle, the mothers to sit and chat or sew. Dinner for mothers and children would be separate, so that the mothers could sit quietly through the meal, and after dinner the sisters would look after the children while the mothers rested. Tea and the evening would be spent as a family, with bed for the children at 7 p.m., and supper for the mothers at 8 p.m. They were then free to walk along the promenade or amuse themselves as they wished until bedtime. A fortnight of this restored many a mother to health and strength and set a family on its feet again.

During the second world war several homes were damaged or bombed, and those that remained were used for families who had been bombed out or were suffering from shock as a result of the injury or death of relatives. A home at Merrow, near Guildford, was used for a short time, but the number of families which could be helped was greatly reduced because of the lack of accommodation.

Once again, after the war, the types of people who used the holiday homes changed. It now became the wives and families of servicemen whose allowances were small, those whose husbands were in prison or unable to support them, and any others who were entirely dependent on national assistance. When the war damage was repaired there were homes at Bexhill, St. Leonards, Southport, Tankerton and Weston-super-Mare, though more recently several of these have had to be closed.

Today, in a more affluent society, most of those who come are sent by welfare workers, the N.S.P.C.C., hospital almoners, local authorities and probation officers, and

more often than not a domestic tragedy lies behind the
desperate need for a holiday and a rest. It may be a young
mother with several children, deserted by her husband, or
a mother exhausted after nursing her husband through a
long illness. But in every case it is a family who could not
otherwise get a holiday, and, unlike most other holiday
homes today, mothers can bring their children with them,
and it is usually possible to give them a room together and
to themselves. The home at Tankerton is now mainly reserved for those who suffer from physical handicaps,
where they can enjoy a holiday in the confidence that the
staff understand their disabilities. This means that for a
time, at least, their loneliness is dispelled and they can
share a holiday with others.

August 1947 saw the opening of the Church Army
Holiday Camp at Seasalter in Kent. The building had
previously been used as a Church Army hut on the common at Southampton, and it was now converted into a
dormitory with fifty-four beds. Ten years later it had become far more palatial.

> There are some six acres of meadows on which stand large
> wooden pavilions, containing the dining-cum-recreation
> room in which are also the chapel, stage and a little camp
> shop, and a line of new shining, streamlined caravans. Part
> of the ground is available for camping in the time-honoured
> style, under canvas.

The camp was at first intended for young people, and
parties of scouts and cubs were among those who used it,
but parochial captains sometimes brought their own local
groups, which would mean a far wider age range. Most of
the people who go to Seasalter today are those who cannot
afford an ordinary holiday. Some are paid for by the
statutory authorities, but many are not and in special
cases the Church Army bears part of the cost. The
Camp tries to give a holiday to families, where, under
ordinary conditions, they would not be able to go away
together.

A rather different type of holiday home is that for clergymen and their families. A note in the *Church Army Review* for 1921 says

> the Church Army owes much to the clergy for their constant and ungrudging help. We are hoping to take in wives and children of very poor clergy in a Clergy Rest House, and so to give them a holiday for which they would otherwise long in vain.

The first home was at Herne Bay, followed by a house at Folkestone, which was rented for a number of years in the summer. In 1926 a house at Clevedon was given to the Church Army for the use of the clergy and their families, and since then, even during the war years, this has been open all the year round for clergy who need a rest. Folkestone has now been superseded by a summer holiday home at Birchington-on-Sea. These two houses now provide annual holidays for more than one hundred clergymen and their wives and children, as well as a small number of lay church workers. Their popularity is such that a family can rarely be accommodated in successive years, and as one of the clergy writes:

> It was not only a restful family holiday, but there was the companionship of others too who had the same ideals and similar problems. My wife spent a whole fortnight without a view of the kitchen sink. The boys had new friends and new places to explore. With the help of snapshots we have re-lived that holiday over and over again.

Church Army officers and their families also needed somewhere for a holiday and a rest, and from the early days a few of the fresh air homes were used for this purpose. Then, just before the first world war, a house at St. Leonards was appropriated for overworked and sick mission-sisters, and a holiday home opened at Southend for married officers and their families. The Sunshine Hospital at Hurstpierpoint, in Sussex, was handed over to the Church Army in 1922. Its wide verandas and beautiful views over the Sussex Downs were just what was needed for a restful holiday, and since that date many Church Army sisters and their friends have enjoyed the benefits of "Sunshine". Two other homes are now available for Church Army personnel—at Ryde in the Isle of Wight, which was once a fresh air home, and at Pevensey Bay in Sussex.

Recently, a new venture has been started in the form of a holiday and conference centre at Carlile Lodge in Folkestone. It is not a holiday home in the usual sense, i.e. for those who cannot afford to pay, but it is a place where parish parties, week-end conferences and holidays for working people can be taken in the most up to date and tasteful surroundings. Its visitors' book reveals a very wide range of people.

These holiday homes, camps and conference centres are greatly needed today in a society whose pace of life is swift and challenging and where periods of rest and relaxation are essential. They are outside the present scope of the welfare state, and are the sort of thing which voluntary organizations are well equipped to do. The Church Army is one of the few voluntary societies which makes it possible for the members of a family to take their holiday as a united group, either in holiday homes where children of all ages are accepted, or at Seasalter, where the father can come as well.

For a time the Church Army came to the help of the family whose mother, for one reason or another, was unable to look after her children. It was a lieutenant of the Royal Navy who in 1915 persuaded the Church Army to take up the cause of the motherless child. He came with the story of the domestic difficulties of a Welsh sapper, Taffy, who, on short leave from fighting in Germany, found his wife in a mental hospital, four of his children in the workhouse, and the fifth, a boy aged seven, missing. The Church Army traced the boy, took the family into its care, and decided this was a form of work which it should do. The holiday home, Hill Brow at Godstone, was taken over for the purpose, and eventually three more homes were added.

When the war ended, it was decided to carry on the work, not only for children of men serving in the forces, but for any child whose mother could not care for it. Many children came to the homes through the medical mission and the sunbeam mission, and in the inter-war period most of the boys were trained for the Merchant Navy, or sent to the Gordon Boys' Home to learn a trade, while the girls were found jobs in domestic service, nursing, and sometimes in social work. The second world war revived the need for these homes for servicemen's children, and once again, when the war was over, other children were accepted. Sometimes the mother was alive, but prolonged physical illness necessitated her absence from home either in a sanatorium or hospital. In other cases the children were without any known relative except the father. But always the father was asked to contribute what he could, and the Church Army made up the rest. As time passed, fewer of these children were in need, for other arrangements were being made for them by the social services, and so one by one these homes have been closed.

THE NEEDS OF THE YOUNGER GENERATION

In youth work, as in so many other aspects of its work, the Church Army has tried to meet needs which were not being satisfied by other organizations. Boys' and girls' clubs were opened in quite large numbers in the late nineteenth century, and so it was only when the Church Army sisters came into contact with girls who did not belong to any existing club that they felt compelled to do something for them. Many of these girls worked in the shops, offices and warehouses around the Edgware Road, and it was for girls from this district that the first club, Heartsease, was started in the early years of this century.

The following is a description of the club when it was first opened.

> The Heartsease Club is managed by a secretary and several Sisters of the Church Army, and it is really a club, quite as much as any of the other clubs in the West End. There is first a pretty and comfortable drawing-room, where you can meet a friend, and enjoy a quiet talk, or listen to the general conversation that is going on. . . . Here and there flowers are dotted about, and, altogether, to a girl whose dwelling is a small bedroom, with only the roofs of other houses to look at, an hour in this room is a tonic in itself. Then, too, if you are wishing to do a little quiet reading or study, there is the writing-room on the ground floor. . . . Next to this room is the Hon. Secretary's private and confidential sitting-room. . . . Here you can take your troubles, your joys, your temptations. But this is not all: like the larger clubs in the West End, you may have your meals there. One of the cosiest of dining-rooms exists down in the basement. Small tables are scattered over the room, so that you can take your meal with the set of friends you have made, and enjoy a quiet midday gossip. Every day a hot dinner can be had for the modest sum of fourpence; and to girls in the West End, who perhaps are a very long distance from home, and unable to afford a good meal in the middle of the day, this is a real blessing. Tea can be had on weekdays, but the brightest meal of the week is, perhaps, tea on Sunday, when, after a short Bible reading, some forty girls file into the dining-room, and all meet for a cup of tea. After tea on Sunday all the company adjourns to the drawing-room, and hymns are sung till it is time for Church.

In 1909 the club moved to the more spacious premises of the old headquarters in the Edgware Road, and was renamed the Alexandra Club. It could now provide bedroom and cubicle accommodation for its members, and this made it possible for those who were temporarily out of work or changing their lodgings to live there, and the sister-in-charge could often help them with the choice of a new job. The junior branch, for girls from fourteen to sixteen, was across the road, and was used by girls from other Church Army homes, or by those out at work for the first time. These girls, as they grew older, would usually transfer their membership to the main club. In the summer many would go to the seaside home at Tankerton for a holiday, and in the winter any who were recovering from an operation or illness could stay there to convalesce.

During the 1920's this club reached its heyday, with about 1,000 members, a tenth of whom were in residence. It became renowned for its evening classes held in the winter, which included sewing, dressmaking, singing and first aid. For several successive years the challenge shield for advanced educational work, which was offered by the Federation of Girls' Clubs, was won, and it was regarded as one of the foremost clubs in London.

A very different type was the Barmaids' Rest, which had been started in a small flat in the Edgware Road in 1903. Barmaids were often shunned by other working girls because it was thought that they associated with men of dubious character. They were employed at very varied hours, and so did not fit into ordinary club life. Thus, there was a need for a club of their own, where they could rest when off duty, have meals at odd hours, and sleep the night if they finished late. The Barmaids' Rest was available for all barmaids and was open from 8 a.m. to midnight. It had rooms where they could read and write, and a sewing room where they could make or renovate their clothes. There was a small dormitory, and a good canteen where food could be obtained at any time. In the late thirties this club became known as the A1 Centre, though it was merely a change in name, for it still provided the same facilities.

After the second world war it was the older married woman who tended to work in the bars, and so the need for the club declined, but it continued in a small way for several years for those who still used it.

Another club which the Church Army ran was the Princess Club in Jamaica Road, Bermondsey, opened in

1907 for the factory girls of the area. Again it differed from the other Church Army clubs and a contemporary account can best describe it.

> Over a shop front, whose windows were whitened beyond the level of the curious eyes of passers-by, "The Princess Club" is painted in red letters on the black name board. The building looks much like its neighbours, except for the opaqued windows, the arresting title, and a few pots of gay flowers on some upper window sills. . . . It has 172 evening members on its books already, besides those who come irregularly; and it also caters for the mid-day needs of from seventy to a hundred girls, most of whom are distinct from the evening members, by providing good, hot dinners at fourpence a head on three days a week during all but the summer months. The Club is primarily intended for a place of cheery and instructive recreation. It opens at 8 p.m. on every weekday evening; and the girls are dismissed, after a brief little service of evening prayers, at 9.45 p.m. In the winter-time there are weekly concerts and a weekly gymnasium class. Every Saturday there is a Temperance class, and a simple hygiene class, or "health talk". On Wednesday there is a short prayer meeting. On Mondays and Wednesdays there is a "Blouse Class" when any one who likes may make pretty blouses for their own wear, under the tuition of kindly lady teachers.

Sunnyland, a similar type of club, was started some ten years later, first at 80 Edgware Road, after which it moved to the Harrow Road. It was a club for "the rough, untrained girls who, with their blokes, swarm noisily in the London street every evening". Open from 7.30 p.m. to 10 p.m. every night, it had the usual games, drill and singing, with buns and tea before closing. As it was near the training home, it was often used to give the sisters in training some experience in club work and management. They would then know how to organize similar clubs when they were on the staff of a parish.

During the first world war there was little provision for the comfort or meals of the girls and young women who replaced men in many of the businesses and warehouses in London, and so the Church Army tried to do something for them. The Rose Restaurant, close to the Alexandra Club, and the Bluebird Room in the rectory of St. Mary-at-Hill, Wilson Carlile's church in the City, were opened to provide lunch and tea at reasonable prices and also rooms where they could wash and rest in their lunch and tea breaks. After the war, when more provision began to be made by firms for their women employees, the Bluebird Room and the Rose Restaurant were closed.

From time to time the Church Army has opened hostels for working girls, particularly when respectable lodgings have been difficult to find in a district, and the level of wages has made it impossible to live further away. One of the first was Mackirdy House, in the Harrow Road, started in 1913 for women and girls earning their living and able to pay a reasonable price for board and lodging. A similar need was met in the 1930's when a hostel was opened in Nelson Square, Blackfriars. More recently, Brookfield House in Eccleston Square was used as a hostel for girls in training or in jobs in London. 1961 marked the opening of Turner House, Primrose Hill, once a home for blind girls, as a hostel for some twenty-five young working girls from Britain and overseas.

> One comes because she has no parents or friends and needs a home rather than the loneliness of "digs". Another is there because an anxious parent likes to know that someone is available if need be. A third can afford only a small amount for living accommodation and would otherwise find herself at the top of some shabby house with only a gas ring to cook on.

Each has her own cubicle bedroom but there are several common rooms where they can meet together and entertain their friends.

The Church Army has never done as much for working boys as it has for girls, probably because at the turn of the century there were many clubs and organizations pro-

vided for them by other voluntary societies. The main
work for boys, in the early years, was through the Boys'
Aid Department, which originally was intended to find
work for school-leavers, but usually befriended any lads in
need. Many of these had parents out of work, and they
themselves were often too inadequately fed and clothed to
feel at home in the various guilds, brigades, scouts or
athletic clubs available in most towns. Therefore the
people who volunteered to help found themselves putting
the lads into touch with some parochial or other organization, helping them to find some suitable evening class
where they would learn a trade, or just offering friendliness
and advice when needed.

By the time the 1920's had arrived, this department had
been closed, but Wilson Carlile was still concerned about
those who were not reached by the uniformed organizations such as scouts, cubs and guides. The situation, now,
was not so much that the children of the poorer streets and
slums were poverty stricken and uncared for, as that they
received little moral or Christian teaching and felt little
responsibility either for themselves or for other people.
During the war their fathers had been away from home,
and their mothers in such a state of anxiety that they
found it difficult to look after their children properly and
to provide a good home background for them.

Mary Burn, the editor of the *Church Army Gazette*, who
had herself run a scouts' group in Acton, had the idea of
the Better Britain Brigade, which should incorporate the
best of the scouts and guides, but with some more definite
Christian teaching. It was welcomed by Wilson Carlile,
and started in 1925. The boys and girls of the Better
Britain Brigades were expected to show obedience, cour-
tesy, kindliness and order in whatever they did, and
they made one promise: "I will try, God helping me, to
leave my Country a better place than I found it". Many
of their activities, such as first aid and home nursing
were similar to those of the scouts and guides, and camps

were organized in the summer so that every child should have at least a fortnight at the sea or in the country. The children in the poorer parishes seemed to enjoy these Brigades, and the captains and sisters found them a most suitable way of providing Christian teaching within a secular setting. They were also useful as a source of recruitment, because some members eventually showed an interest in working with the Church Army.

By the end of the second world war the need for a distinctive organization for the children of poorer parents was no longer necessary, as children were now in a more equal social position. The only need for the Better Britain Brigades was to supply the spiritual teaching which had been so important a part of their work. Therefore in the autumn of 1945 agreements were reached between the Church Army and the Boy Scouts' and Girl Guides' Associations to recognize Church Army scout troops and guide companies which should include in their badge work some definite religious teaching. So the Better Britain Brigades came to an end and their members became part of the scout and guide movement.

The Church Army is now represented in the higher ranks of scouting and guiding, and the Church Army scouts and guides come under the district commissioners of the local associations in the usual way. The only difference is that the scouters and guiders of groups connected with Church Army have to be communicant members of the Church of England. Allegiance to the Church Army by the scouts and guides themselves is shown in the Church Army badge, which they wear in addition to the usual badges, and in the crusader badge which is granted for Christian allegiance. Camping is a very important part of their programme, for it provides them with the opportunity for showing initiative and taking responsibility, which is often lacking in their everyday life. The cubs use the Seasalter Camp, and the guides have recently gone to Danny Park, Hurstpierpoint. The scouts sometimes venture abroad on a fortnight's trip to Europe, which helps them to make friends with young people in other countries.

Youth work has also changed in character since the twenties and thirties. Young people are now rarely in need of material help, but are often greatly in need of advice. They question the standards accepted by their parents, but do not know what to put in their place. They rightly wish to manage their own affairs, but are not always entirely successful in doing so. Thus a changed approach is needed on the part of those who run the clubs, and a change is needed as well in club activities. What was suitable thirty years ago would no longer go down. Furthermore, the State has taken a far greater interest in the needs of youth, and, though leaving the practical aspects to voluntary organizations, has suggested lines of approach which should be followed.

The Youth Committee at Church Army headquarters, in 1943, arranged a training week in London for twenty-five captains and sisters from all over the country to see something of the changes taking place in other clubs and settlements and to reconsider the place of Christian leadership in the youth service. This new approach led to the starting of house parties for young people and the opening of youth centres.

The first experimental youth house party was held at the end of 1945, and proved a popular means whereby young people could take a holiday, meet other people and discuss the problems which particularly concerned them. The youth centres fulfilled a different purpose, for they were intended to be places where young people could congregate in the evenings for pleasure and amusement. They were more in the nature of an informal club which young people could attend when they felt in the mood, play games and chat. They were also places where the young person who did not fit into any of the regular organizations would be accepted and feel at home. Therefore they were very variable in form, and had to be adapted to meet the needs of the area which they covered.

The youth centre at Chaddesdon, Derby, had been run by the vicar himself before the Church Army captain arrived, but the captain could give his whole attention to it. The centre, which was a disused Army hut, soon had some four hundred members and was open every evening from 4.30 until 10. Each age group occupied the centre for a certain length of time each day, and had its own committee of boys and girls who were in full charge and arranged the programmes. When the session for one particular age group was up they would sweep the hut ready for the next. Meanwhile, those waiting their turn either danced or chatted or listened to the inevitable juke box, which for a small coin not only played all the latest tunes but also made a small profit for the club. Asked what they had done before the organization of the centre, the members replied, "Hung around the streets and got into trouble." The captain kept very much in the background. He had shown the members how to run the club and they were running it. His job was to be there when wanted, but not to interfere.

The Fleetwood Youth Centre has an entirely different approach.

> In the youth centre at Fleetwood, no pretence is made concerning the Christian faith. Nothing is wrapped up and presented with hands clad in boxing gloves. Right from the entry of the boy or girl into the club evidence is to be seen of our faith. The notice board boldly advertises Bible Study; club epilogue and prayers every night; the beautiful chapel where periodically we meet round the altar for the Eucharistic feast; the word of advice; the discipline; the fun and jokes; the corporate venture; preparation for citizenship. . . . These can be and are done with a Christian basis. We are concerned with the *whole* of a youngster, not *just a part*!

The Crossed Swords Club in Lorrimore Square, Southwark, forms part of the rebuilding of St. Paul's, Walworth, which was badly blitzed, and it shares the ground floor of the new church building with the social centre, which has a dance floor, coffee bar and play rooms, with facilities for floodlit tennis, netball, and football practice. In a community of 12,000, who are largely flat-dwellers, the club and social centre try to bring the people together. As the vicar says: "The vision here is one of a common meeting ground, where in cultural, social and physical re-creation, we may together (and the togetherness is important) rediscover that most important part of man's make-up, the spiritual."

Much of the less obvious work of the Church Army is done not only through these youth centres and the other organizations for young people, but also through the informal gatherings which so often take place in the captain's or sister's flat, and which may be the first introduction which the boy or girl has to Christian teaching. Thus youth work forms an important part in the training of the Church Army officer, for there are few jobs which he or she will be required to do which do not have some connexion with young people. It is especially important in parish work where the captain or sister is nearly always responsible for the Sunday school and for the other young people's organizations.

IN AND OUT OF PRISON

People who are sent to prison often find themselves in need of help. They are not always very wise people in the first place; their families have to do without them usually at a time when the income of the father is greatly needed; and when they come out of prison there are many problems of adjustment to be faced. The Church Army has always had the welfare of the prisoner and his family very much at heart. We read in the annual report of 1888 that a Church Army officer would spend part of his time at the prison gate "for it is there, just when the convict has to face the world and his old comrades on his discharge, that he needs a warm heart and a loving hand".

At that time the official policy was that, as far as possible, the prisoner should be cut off from the world outside. Prison visiting was not encouraged, and, apart from his fellow prisoners, the only people whom a man would meet would be the prison officers and the chaplain. This meant that, if he had been in prison any length of time, when he did come out he would probably have lost touch with his family and would feel completely lost in an unfamiliar world. There were Discharged Prisoners' Aid societies from which he could get help, but he was more likely to seek out his old friends and either end up in prison again, or be forced to take refuge in the casual ward of the workhouse. Church Army officers would come across men who had been in prison when they visited the workhouses, and for a time workhouse and prison work were linked together as one department of the Society.

The main help which the Church Army could offer in these very early days was in their labour homes, and ex-prisoners were encouraged to go to them. Sometimes the prison governor would allow a little card to be fixed in the cells giving the name of the nearest Church Army labour home. If the man made good in the labour home, work would be found for him, or he might be recommended for emigration.

Sir E. J. Ruggles-Brise, at that time chairman of the Prison Commission, said at a meeting in 1896: "I am glad to show the obligation which I feel towards the Society. The Church Army Labour Homes are doing a good work in connexion with our prisons. There are now twenty-four Labour Homes connected with prisons; but there are thirty-two without a Labour Home. We should like to have a Labour Home to each prison."

But it was essential, if any widespread help was to be given to prisoners, to have some contact with them while they were in prison. Therefore the Church Army was very pleased when, in 1897, the Home Office granted a request for a prison mission to be held in Wandsworth prison. Captain Davey, who was at that time on "central duty", which meant that he kept himself ready for any special efforts of an evangelistic nature, was sent. He not only preached each evening in the prison chapel, but he was allowed the great privilege of an interview, in the presence of a warder, with any prisoner who wanted to see him. Captain Spencer, who for many years was connected with prison work, was then sent to conduct a similar mission in Pentonville, and within eighteen months missions had been held in thirty-four prisons.

The prison mission usually started on a Sunday and lasted for eight days. Each day the missioner would either take the whole service or give the address. Often he was allowed to visit from cell to cell before the mission, and to have private interviews with those who wanted to see him during the mission. He might then return after a few months to renew his acquaintance with those who had been interested. Work within the prisons was always somewhat restricted, but gradually the mission services were made less formal, and occasionally a Church Army choir might be invited to lead the singing. Yet it was 1917 before the first lantern service was permitted, and 1955 before a film mission was held in Wormwood Scrubbs prison. Nowadays, missions within the prisons are conducted in a less formal manner, but there obviously cannot be the same amount of freedom as at a similar service outside.

Church Army captains gradually became regular visitors at the prisons, and were able to supplement much of what the chaplain was doing. They had the advantage of being laymen, and were usually more familiar with the background from which the prisoner came and so were able to understand his problems. They also had the departments of the Church Army behind them, and could call upon varied sources of help. For example:

H

in one cell was a man who had heard his daughter was missing. The information was passed to a Church Army sister, who was fortunate enough to find the daughter in a far-away town. The next cell contained an old soldier. His medals were in pawn and would be irretrievably lost within a few days. A Church Army officer saved the medals. In the next cell was a man grievously worried about his wife. According to the man's story their child should have been born a month before the Church Army officer's visit. The Church Army Prisoners' families' department secured touch with the woman, found that the child had not yet been born, and added a message that they would help in every possible way. The fourth man was troubled because his fiancée was out of work through her association with him. Employment was found for her away from the neighbourhood.

A Church Army prison evangelist was appointed as a lay helper to one of the chaplains for the first time in 1910, and in 1914 a resident evangelist was attached to Parkhurst prison. Since then Church Army captains have been on the staff of several of the larger prisons, and many visit in the local gaols. By 1950 Church Army workers assisted the chaplains in Wormwood Scrubbs, Dartmoor, Parkhurst, Wandsworth, Holloway, Pentonville, Walton, Wakefield, Armley and Durham. Describing a day's work in one of these prisons, a Church Army officer writes:

> There are the many visits to make, both in the cells and Hospital and letters to write so that help for the individual prisoner can be obtained. The Captain or Sister has various committees to attend. They also arrange services and classes, and often conduct the prisoners' choir practice, and do many other jobs which mean so much to the prisoners concerned.

These jobs include such things as preparing candidates for confirmation, leading discussion groups and planning entertainments, all of which help to make the prisoner feel that he is a person, and that somebody cares for him.

Church Army sisters were also visiting the women in Holloway and Aylesbury prisons by 1910, and today they, too, are chaplain's assistants. The work of a sister in a prison is very similar to that of a captain. She holds Bible classes and services on Sundays, but her main task is with the women's personal welfare, and she aims at being their friend and helping them to get back their self-respect.

"I have to win their confidence before I can help them. I have to try to break down their opposition, give them comfort, sometimes scold them, and often advise and help them," says one of the sisters who was chaplain's assistant in the women's prison at Strangeways.

The wives and families of prisoners probably received help from the Church Army at an earlier date than prisoners themselves, for any sister, in her visiting, would have been bound to come across them. Not only were they usually short of money, but they were often shunned by their neighbours and ashamed to ask for help. By 1898 the Church Army was organizing a system of relief in the form of money, food, clothes and work. The usual method at the time was to make it possible for the wife to earn some money. She might be supplied with a mangle so that she could take in washing, or a sewing-machine to do simple work for a clothing factory. Sometimes she was given flowers, fruit or vegetables to sell in the streets; or pieces of material to make up into garments for her family.

The first centrally organized help for prisoners' wives was in 1908 when a workroom was opened in Highbury Grove. Various forms of work were provided, according to the ability of the woman. There was laundering, fine needlework, the making of hassocks and church kneelers, rag sorting for paper manufacture, and other simple tasks; but whatever work she did, she received the same daily wage and three free meals. Meanwhile her young children were cared for in a nursery close to the workroom.

After the first world war, help for prisoners' families was organized from headquarters. Application for help would come from chaplains and governors of prisons, social workers, the clergy, other Church Army workers, friends and relatives of prisoners, and sometimes from the prisoners themselves. A prisoner would often confide to the chaplain his desperate worry about the state of his family. The chaplain would get into touch with the Church Army, who would visit them and see what could be done.

"To be able to send back a message that the home is being maintained; that the wife is bravely carrying on; that the children are doing well" has often been a turning point in the prisoner's attitude to life.

When the Church Army was put into touch with a family, a sister would either visit or write a friendly letter asking the wife to call at headquarters. Rarely would she visit in uniform, for that might reveal the situation to curious neighbours. Sometimes the rent would be paid for a few weeks until the woman had time to adjust herself to the situation. Work might have to be found, clothing provided for herself and her children, since much might have already been pawned, and debts paid. Employment in the Church Army workrooms might be a solution, but it would depend upon the ages of the children and the length of the man's sentence.

The welfare state has not made a great difference to the needs of prisoners' families, for, although national assistance can be claimed and therefore the family is not destitute, rent is likely to be in arrears, hire-purchase payments unmet, and gas and electricity disconnected. The housing situation and the threat of eviction place many families in a difficult situation, and hostel accommodation has frequently to be found for them. But much of the sister's work is still personal. A father or mother may be broken-hearted because their child has been detained. Husband and wife may drift apart while the man is in prison, and the sister has to pave the way for the wife to visit him and to accept him when he comes out. A woman may leave her children with relatives or neighbours, without any indication that she is going into Holloway. All these and many

similar situations may have to be met by the Church
Army sister.

One of the most critical times in the life of a prisoner is
the moment of discharge. Discharged Prisoners' Aid
societies had been, since 1862, the recognized means of
helping the prisoner on release, and in 1900 the Church
Army was granted this recognition. This was largely due
to the success of its existing work for prisoners, since for
two years a special home had been available in Leeds for
star class prisoners, and a lodging house for the newly discharged. Arrangements were made to find work for the
men, usually with some understanding employer who was
willing to take them and help them over the initial difficulties. When the Church Army became recognized as one
of these Discharged Prisoners' Aid societies it was much
easier for it to help prisoners, as a special staff of Church
Army officers was allowed to visit each of the prisons with
which the Church Army was connected every six months,
and to interview those who were due for discharge in the
near future. Prison missions helped to make the prisoners
familiar with the work of the Church Army and many
were rehabilitated through its services.

When, in 1910, new legislation provided for convicts on
ticket-of-leave to report to a Discharged Prisoners' Aid
society, many chose the Church Army. This meant a close
contact with such men before they were finally discharged,
and the opportunity of finding employment for them in
advance. But it was not an easy task, for some of the most
dangerous criminals were involved. Those who could not
be placed in permanent employment at once were accepted
in the labour homes and lodging homes on a par with the
other men until work could be found for them, and when
they left the captain continued to keep in touch with them.

The method of helping the ex-prisoner has not altered
greatly. The Church Army may be able to find or give
him employment or provide him with special equipment
which will enable him to work. If there is no Church

Army hostel in the district where he works, then he may be given a grant to pay for his lodgings until he draws his first week's pay, and as a matter of course he will be put in touch with the local vicar or any Church Army officer that may be in the area. There are failures as well as successes but many who might otherwise have returned to prison "go straight".

Sisters have helped women prisoners on release in a similar manner. For many years the Red House, Bootle, near Walton Prison, offered a temporary home to the woman who had just been released until she could decide what the next step should be, and it also housed for the night countless relatives of prisoners who were to be discharged the next day. Likewise, in London, the sister at Belvedere House would visit Holloway regularly, and "put up" any ex-prisoner who needed lodgings.

For many years, the Church Army had a hut outside Wormwood Scrubbs prison, with a sister in charge, and a constant supply of cups of tea and light refreshments. The hut would be used in the early morning by the relatives of those who were to be discharged that day, and the friendly smile and kindly words of the sister helped many an ex-prisoner and his wife before they left. A prisoner with no friend or relative to meet him would usually trudge uncertainly across to the hut, and find himself provided with "a nice cup of tea", a cake and cigarette, interspersed with much sympathy and sound advice. In the afternoons the hut would be used by those visiting their menfolk in prison. They might want some refreshment or support while waiting for the time of admission, and they would often look in on their way out for comfort or help.

At one time young people went to prison in the same way as adults, but it gradually became customary for them to be placed on probation. The Probation of Offenders' Act of 1907 made probation available for most offences, and empowered magistrates to appoint probation officers. Before this, the Church Army had sometimes been asked by the courts to supervise young people who had committed some small offence, and so, when the Act came into force, twelve Church Army captains and sisters, who had been involved in this work, were appointed as probation officers by the authorities.

Probation is a method of dealing with a person who has been found guilty of an offence, but who, instead of going to prison, is placed under the supervision of a probation officer, and allowed to live in the community under certain conditions of conduct imposed by the court. The duty of the probation officer has always been to keep in touch with such a person, and to "advise, assist and befriend him". This means helping to build up his character, and Church Army personnel have always been well equipped for such work.

Sometimes a probation order contained a condition of residence, making it necessary for the person to live in a special home or hostel. Lads' hostels, in connexion with the labour homes at Maidstone and Leicester, were used for this purpose in the early years of this century. First offenders were sent to them by the magistrates instead of to prison, and they were always available for lads of sixteen to twenty-one on leaving gaol. In each case the lads' hostel was separate from the labour home and lodging house, and in that part of the building occupied by the captain and his wife, so that they could keep a friendly eye on them. It was usual to employ the lads, at first, in the hostel on housework, wood-chopping, or carpentry, and later, when they had proved their worth, to send them out to daily work in the district.

Between the two world wars the numbers of young people on probation increased, and the Church Army opened another two probation hostels, one in the Marylebone Road for young fellows between the ages of eighteen and twenty-five, and a second at Sutton Veny, near Warminster. The latter was for younger lads who were capable of learning a trade, and in these country surroundings they were taught poultry farming and market gardening. For a time the hostel at Stonebridge Park was used as a probation hostel, and part of the buildings at the Hempstead Hall Farm as a remand home for lads awaiting a vacancy at an approved school.

Young people, convicted of an offence but not placed on probation, have been sent, since the middle of the nineteenth century, to reformatories, or approved schools as they are now called. In the past, most Church Army moral welfare workers were also part-time probation officers, and this brought them into touch with girls convicted by the courts. Thus, the Church Army, through its moral welfare work, found itself involved in starting reformatories for girls.

The first of these was Queen Elizabeth Lodge at Southgate, which was used as a reformatory in 1915. Girls who were unsuitable for the ordinary reformatory either because of their past experiences, or on account of the depths to which they had sunk, were sent there. In fact, it was known as the place to which those who were too bad for any other home were sent. Parkside, at Huyton near Liverpool, was the second reformatory, and was opened in 1917 for girls with less serious offences and with a better home background. In 1920 the Church Army took over the control of the Stafford County Home, for those in need of care and protection as well as for girls from the courts. As was usual at this period, a training in domestic service was given, though for a time Queen Elizabeth Lodge specialized in hand weaving, and Parkside in making toys, and a delightful little shop in Kensington Church Street sold their products to the public.

The girl who was sent to an approved school after the second world war was often the product of her home background. A sister in charge of one of the Church Army approved schools says:

Most of the girls who come to us are from broken homes or homes where no moral training is given, and many of them have previously had no specific teaching or a decent standard of living. They have only known quarrelling and swearing, barely-furnished and ill-kept homes, with no regularity of meals and no discipline except when parents are irritated in some way by the children's behaviour. In some cases mother or father has intimate associations with the opposite sex and the children have been brought up to think that this is the normal way of life. Some of the girls become friendly with those who lead them into a life of crime and larceny, and this is a common cause of committal to a school. Many have been brought up in institutions or homes because they were unwanted as children. Each of them needs patience, love and understanding before the barriers of bitterness and hardship which they have erected against the outside world can be broken down.

The emphasis was now on helping the girls to live as members of the community, and during the time they spent with the Church Army they were taught the value of money, how to care for their clothes, and generally to live as responsible people. When they were ready to go out to work, suitable work was found for them, many of them being employed in laundries, factories, guest houses, shops and offices. In the 1950's the Church Army had two approved schools, Parkside and Bryanston House in Nottingham. But with the changing pattern of work for approved schools and child care they have both been closed.

The members of the prison welfare department are now principally engaged in helping the chaplains with their pastoral work, and the families of those in prison. Other Church Army officers in their daily work are constantly meeting those who have been in prison, and are able to give them the support and advice which they so often need, and make them feel that they are accepted members of the community.

The whole purpose of Church Army work for the so-called delinquent has been to give him or her a chance. In the past it was a chance to live in decent surroundings and

to hold a worthwhile and secure job. Now it is a chance to
fit into and be accepted by the community.

SOMEWHERE TO LIVE

The Archbishop of York, in his foreword to *Roof Over-
head! Twenty-five Years of Church Army Housing*, wrote in
1951:

> The Church has always been deeply concerned about home
> life, but for very large numbers of our fellow countrymen
> the shortage of houses has made a normal home life impos-
> sible; they are compelled to live either in conditions which
> are grossly overcrowded, in which privacy is impossible, or
> in houses which long ago should have been demolished.
> Many young married couples are also living with their
> parents, an arrangement which does not always prove
> satisfactory. Great efforts have been made by the State to
> cope with a problem which is gigantic in its extent, and a
> solution of which is essential for the well-being of the nation.

For a long time housing for families with low incomes
has been a serious problem, and one which was almost
completely ignored by the State until after the first world
war. Several trusts and beneficent persons built cottages
and tenements for working people in the latter years of the
nineteenth and in the early twentieth century, but these
went very little way to meet the great need. Church Army
captains and sisters would often find, in their visiting, that
difficulties were aggravated by the overcrowding and in-
sanitary conditions of many of the dwellings in which
these people lived. The following is an extract from a
report of a Church Army sister who visited homes in the
East End of London in the early twenties:

> The poor things live in a sort of hut made on four legs. It
> is not high enough for them to stand up in, and there is not
> room for even a table. They have made up a bed in it—no
> bedstead—which comes to the door. They sit on the end of

this, and this acts as a chair. There is nothing to heat the place properly; the only fire they have being an old water tank with a bucket of fire put inside. Unless they keep the door open they see nothing. It is most distressing, and both seem such nice people, and the child is a little picture. They are very clean personally; poor things they have been really hungry.

The Church Army would probably have regarded the building of houses for such people as outside its terms of reference, particularly in the 1920's when the local authorities for the first time were given certain powers with regard to house building, had it not been for Mrs. Sowton Barrow of Exmouth who, on return to England after several months abroad, was struck by the deplorable conditions in which she found people living in the big cities. In July, 1924, hearing that a women's demonstration was to be held at the Queen's Hall, Langham Place, to call for more energetic action in dealing with this housing problem, she travelled up from Devon, with a cheque in her purse, hoping that she would discover some suitable scheme for building houses for needy families. All the meeting accomplished was to put pressure on councils and public bodies to increase their housing programmes, but what Mrs. Sowton Barrow succeeded in doing was to meet Wilson Carlile. Finding that he was deeply interested in the matter she agreed to go and see him the next morning. After talking with him she offered him the cheque, but with the proviso that if the Church Army did not have a working scheme within two months it should be returned to her. Wilson Carlile used to tell, with a chuckle, how a lady bullied him into building houses, and held a pistol, in the form of a cheque, at his head.

Thus far the Church Army had concentrated upon social work for people in need. A housing project would be an entirely new venture, since it would involve the receiving and spending of large sums of money for a particular purpose. The Church Army board felt that it could not reject such an offer outright; on the other hand it would find difficulty in incorporating such a scheme within the ordinary administration of the Church Army. Therefore, it was decided to form a separate society, with separate funds—the Church Army Housing Limited—which in November, 1924, was registered as a public utility company. Sir Frank Elgood agreed to become chairman, and the officials of the new society were chosen from among the Church Army general committee or the Church Army board. Sir Frank was already closely connected with the Church Army, for he had served as commissioner for the Church Army during the first world war, and then became co-treasurer. He was also well-known as an architect and authority on housing matters, since for a time he had been housing commissioner under the Ministry of Health, and later chairman of the National Housing and Town Planning Council.

The company started with £15,000 in donations, and £3,000 on loan, and this was enough, at that time, to build sixty houses at a cost of £600 each, the Church Army paying £300, and the other £300 being advanced by the local authorities on the security of the rents. It was only a small venture in a very large field, but

> feeling very deeply the reproach to Christianity which the continuance of evil housing conditions present, the Housing Society was formed with the principal purpose of being able to show how Christian voluntary bodies may do something practical towards the solution of this grave problem, which is one of the main sources of social and spiritual discontent.

The houses were intended for large families from bad living conditions, and for the first six years only families with five or more children who were living in one room were accepted, with a preference for ex-service men. The first tenant to go into one of these new houses was a Mrs. Angel who had six children and a shell-shocked husband. After being turned out of their one-roomed dwelling, they had lived in the workhouse until a Church Army sister had befriended them and recommended them for Church Army rehousing.

The first site was Church Army land adjoining the Stonebridge Park hostel for men and boys, and here twelve cottages were erected, each with front and back gardens, three bedrooms, a living-room, scullery and bathroom. Most of the new tenants found it impossible to furnish such spacious quarters after their one-roomed dwellings, so the Church Army usually had to help them from its stocks of furniture which people had donated.

Wilson Carlile felt that more wealthy people should recognize their responsibility towards their less fortunate neighbours by helping them in this way, and so he tried to get local churches and groups of Christian people to contribute towards the cost of such dwellings. The next scheme, which was in Walworth on land leased from the Ecclesiastical Commissioners, was supported by the congregation of the church of St. Edmund, King and Martyr, Lombard Street, whose rector, the Rev. J. Studdert Kennedy, was known to many as "Woodbine Willie". They met the cost of eight of the sixteen flats which were built. Similarly, at Croydon, St. Peter's subscribed enough for two of the four houses to be built there.

This method of building was also encouraged in provincial towns. A small committee would be formed to publicize the need and collect financial backing. Then a few houses would be built, with the expectation that others would follow. This plan was most successful in Exeter, where within ten years the number of cottages built was increased from eight to thirty, a few of them almost under the shadow of the cathedral. Mrs. Sowton Barrow was largely responsible for this rapid development, and her committee not only raised the necessary funds, but also managed the property for several years. Other places where similar development took place were Farnham Common, Buckinghamshire, where two cottages were built in response to a request from a donor; Lanark, where a family of supporters enabled twenty-four houses to be built; and Perth, where a Scottish donor from India sponsored twenty houses.

One of the largest groups of cottages to be constructed in the twenties was at Winchmore Hill, Southgate, where fifty-six three and four-bedroom dwellings were built, in pairs and short terraces, forming a whole street. The *Palmers Green Gazette* said at that time:

> In providing dwellings at Barrow Close, Winchmore Hill, for people who formerly had existed in sordid surroundings, Church Army Housing did excellent work. They gave parents an opportunity for caring for their children in an environment that was sure to be beneficial and of far-reaching effect in their physical and moral development.

A mission hut and welfare centre were given by a lady well-wisher, and a supervisor's house built in addition to the existing cottages.

Property of this size needed careful and skilful management, and at first trained housing managers were employed. But as well as collecting the rent and attending to repairs and improvements to the property, they had to face problems such as failure to pay the rent, dirt and bug infestation, and disputes between tenants. It was found that the captains and sisters who lived near, with the help of lady visitors, were most successful in solving these. Therefore housing managers were replaced by rent-collectors who were helped by Church Army officers and by honorary welfare visitors. Thus it was possible to create a sense of responsibility which no doubt accounted for the small number of families which had to be evicted.

A captain, who had gone to reside on an estate where there were some rather troublesome tenants, was asked how he had attained such speedy and remarkable results. His reply was, "Oh! just living with them."

Sites in the central parts of London were too small to permit the building of cottages, and so flats had to be considered. Sir Frank Elgood wanted to avoid as far as possible the construction of high blocks with the difficulties of stairs for women with young children, and so he devised a three-storey building consisting of one ground floor flat and two maisonettes above, each with its own street door and with living-rooms on the first floor and bedrooms on the second. With only two exceptions, this type of building was used in Central London. Southwark was the first example, where twelve of these "cottage-flats" were built on the corner of Tabard and Weston Streets in 1928, to be followed by twenty-four more, which included a block named after the chairman, Elgood House. *The Church Times* reporting the opening ceremony writes:

> Tabard Street was quite excited. At the first-floor window of the "pub" across the road, a family gathering was busy snapping the Bishop's gaiters and the scarlet and fur of His Worship the Mayor. On the roof of the neighbouring factory, a long row of cheering men and boys was outlined against the sky; while all the workmen employed on the building eagerly watched the proceedings. Houses near the men's work, that was what appealed most to the mothers of Southwark. More even than for cheap rents and coal cupboards and bathrooms.

The Church Army always sought the co-operation of local authorities in finding sites, in obtaining loans for part of the cost of the building, and in securing whatever government subsidy might be available. Advice was sought from local authority technical officials, and the mayor and other municipal officers were invited to the opening ceremony. But it was always a difficult task to choose from the long list of applicants the families who were in the greatest need and were also suitable for the three and four-bedroom dwellings. In practically all cases they were families that few landlords or municipalities cared to accept, either because they were too poor to pay the required rent, or because they came from one-roomed cellars and rat-ridden dwellings which were not yet condemned by the authorities and so their inhabitants stood little chance of being helped by their own local council.

The Housing Act of 1930 placed emphasis upon slum clearance, and therefore councils began to rehouse the people from this type of area. The Church Army followed a similar policy and gave preference to families living in the slums, without regard necessarily to the number of children. This meant providing dwellings which would take families of various sizes, rather than the three and four-bedroom houses on which they had previously concentrated. The property at Coldharbour Lane, Lambeth, was an example of this new policy. The site had been bought from the Ecclesiastical Commissioners and had more than forty old houses on it, which were reconditioned and reconstructed to bring them up to the standards required by Church Army Housing.

Fifty-two flats, in two blocks, were built on the adjoining piece of spare land, and they were the first departure from the cottage-flat principle, since they consisted of four floors instead of three, but had a balcony on the first floor from which were entrances to maisonettes on the second and third floors. One block was called Canterbury Close and the other York Close as a reminder that they were built "in response to the call of the Archbishops for the better housing of the people", and this was inscribed upon the corner stone which was laid by the Archbishop of Canterbury in January, 1934. A similar construction was used for flats in Kensington and in Kennington.

Other types of dwellings were built in the thirties. At Camberwell part of the property was used for shops, garages and sheds, the rents of which helped to finance the low-rented dwellings. The West Drayton cottages near the Paddington and Birmingham canal were occupied by families who had previously lived entirely on the barges. At the estates at Gateshead, and later at Enfield, special arrangements were made for old people to live near their families in small flats, with a bedroom, living-room, bathroom and kitchen, and lawns where they could sit out in warm weather. At Mitcham, six cottages with covered verandas, known as "sunshine houses", were built for families where a member was threatened with tuberculosis.

By this time the Church Army had built over eight hundred houses, but with the coming of war, building had to stop, and policy with regard to new tenants was changed to meet wartime needs. A report presented to the annual meeting of Church Army Housing says:

> At the time of and after air raids in London we have promptly offered to the Authorities all available accommodation for rehousing bombed-out families. Advantage has been taken of this, particularly in East and South-East London. All vacancies are allotted through the billeting officers to such families, apart from a few which were offered to the families of men serving in H.M. Forces who needed specially low-rented houses. Approximately sixty bombed families have been rehoused by us, i.e. over 10 per cent of our London tenants. Among these are people who have been bombed out twice, and even three times, but who, with unflagging courage, have started new homes with what they could buy with their limited compensation money, perhaps a few possessions saved from the wreckage, and in some cases with aid from our Tenants' Welfare Fund.

The later years of the war brought greater devastation and destruction and, on one estate in London, half of the thirty-six houses were completely destroyed, and most of the rest rendered uninhabitable. Rents were difficult to collect because tenants were evacuated; much of the property was left untended and hooligans could easily break in during the blackout.

By the end of the war, almost all the property in London had received some damage, and that which was habitable required much renovation and repair. Although the government paid for the restoration of war-damaged property, costs of repair and maintenance had risen greatly. A major increase was in the cost of labour, and this made

I

it impossible for Church Army Housing to undertake interior decorating. Instead, allowances were made to tenants for materials, so that they could do their own. Rents were controlled by the Rent Restriction Acts, and this caused some strange anomalies between tenants. It also made it difficult to persuade families which had grown smaller to move to more suitable accommodation. As to new building, it was almost impossible to obtain a licence, and increasingly costly to build. Therefore Church Army Housing, in the immediate post-war years, had to reconsider its policy.

Even before the war had ended, it had been suggested that the two most needy groups were young married couples without a home of their own, and the elderly who had been bombed out or evacuated, and had nowhere to which to return. Therefore, when the war ended; it was these groups, along with the families of ex-service men whose homes had been destroyed, which received most attention.

A certain amount of building did take place in the post-war years. Twelve family flats with two, three and four bedrooms, were built at Hackney. At Camberwell, work on an estate which had started before the war was completed. Here, the Church Army included six one-roomed flatlets, which were let to young married couples without children, who had no chance of a place on any housing list and had insufficient income to pay the rent charged by private landlords. In the mid-fifties, a large block of eighty-two flats of varying sizes was erected at Lambeth to replace property purchased in the thirties and now beyond repair. Some of the previous tenants were rehoused but, since one-third of the flats were small, it was possible to let them to elderly people, or to those just married.

Since then no new building has taken place, and Church Army Housing has devoted much of its resources to modernizing the houses on existing estates. Many were built more than thirty years ago, and have become out of date by modern standards. Such things as the replacement of gas lighting by electricity, new fireplaces, the renovation of bathrooms, and modernizing of kitchens have all had to be done. Gardens have been replanned, and the lawns of a block of flats in North Kensington have been converted into a playground for children who are too young for school.

Church Army Housing has now about nine hundred and fifty family dwellings under its control. These are only a minute proportion of the number of low rent dwellings provided by the local authorities and other voluntary housing associations. But they are something towards the great need, which still exists, of homes for families with low incomes. Church Army Housing showed that the Church was aware of one of the most urgent social problems of the inter-war period, and their houses still stand to demonstrate this. Since 1945 the main activity of Church Army Housing has been in providing flatlets for the elderly, and this Churchill Scheme, as it is called, will form part of the next section.

RETIREMENT AND ITS PROBLEMS

The population of this country is often described as an ageing one. From the beginning of the century the proportion of old people has been gradually increasing and is to-day more than double what it was in 1901. Families were larger in the early years of the century, and so more people are now in the older age groups, and great advances in medicine have lengthened the expectation of life. An old person of eighty is no longer a rarity and many live to a greater age. The pattern of living has also changed. With difficulties in housing and married women going out to work, the old cannot always be cared for by their children, who often feel no responsibility towards them. Thus the needs of the elderly have become an increasingly serious problem.

In the early years of the century it was customary for old people without means, unless they were fortunate enough to qualify for a place in an almshouse, to end their days in the workhouse. Then, in 1908, an old-age pension was granted to such people who were seventy or over, and this helped them to live a little longer on their own. But, even then, they could afford to pay very little rent, and were often obliged to live in abject penury. The Church Army captains and sisters would visit them in their homes or in the workhouse, and try to do what they could to make their lives a little more happy. In the year when pensions were first granted, we read in the *Review*:

> There are in the slums old, infirm people who never cross the threshold because they cannot walk; so they sit in their one little room, very often patiently and hopefully from year's end to year's end. To some of these poor old folk we send men with Bath chairs, to give them an hour or two's airing in the parks, so that they can see the trees and flowers, and feel the sunshine for a while. The parks seem nothing very wonderful to us. After years spent, night and day, in a small back room in a small back street, they look like paradise.

The Church Army always accepted old people in their lodging houses, and made special arrangements for them. The pensioners' room would be set aside where, if they wished, they could sit all day in easy chairs, around a blazing fire. The price of a bed was lower for them than for the ordinary lodger, and sometimes there were pensioners' dormitories. Since they had little money for food and other small items, meals could be bought at the canteen at cheaper prices, and sometimes they could cook or reheat food which they brought in from outside. They were treated not as mere lodgers but as members of the family, and, when they needed clothing or footwear or stronger spectacles, headquarters managed to supply them. The old people paid what they could towards their lodging, but this would be supplemented from the Old

People's Fund, so that the lodging houses would not run at a deficit. Elderly people are still to be found in the men's and women's hostels, and they are happy because they are able to live their own lives and feel secure under the oversight of the captain or sister in charge, who notices when they have some little ailment, and is able to make arrangements if they need the help of the social services.

In the depression of the late twenties many who sought help were elderly married people who were not capable of living on their own. Therefore it was decided to turn the children's home at Fleet into a home for married couples, both of whom were over the age of sixty. This led the Church Army to consider opening separate homes for elderly men and for elderly women who did not feel happy living in the ordinary hostels. They became known as anchorage homes for men, and sunset homes for women, and were designed to provide the freedom they would expect in an ordinary guest house. The men and women paid what they could manage but any excess was met from the Old People's Fund.

Anchorage homes have always been fewer than sunset homes, because there are fewer elderly men needing somewhere to live. The home at Fleet, with another at Tunbridge Wells, which had been started in 1920 for non-uniformed Church Army pensioners, and a small home at Brighton, constituted the total of anchorage homes until 1949, when a new home at Newcastle was added. By 1955 their number had increased to six, with nearly a hundred men living in them. There are now four, two of them in Brighton, another in County Durham, and the original home, Court Moor, at Fleet.

The residents come from very different walks of life, though as far as possible those with similar backgrounds are placed together. Each has his "fatigue" to do, usually some small job of polishing or dusting, which he reckons he does better than any woman, but he is free to amuse himself for the rest of the time as he likes. Many play chess, dominoes and darts, and most are keen critics of the local football and cricket. A few are able to do gardening and have tiny plots in the garden of the home. But this was too elementary for one old gentleman, who arrived with a large spade shining like silver. For ten years he spent many happy hours digging in a near-by allotment.

The emergency shelter at Boniface Street, which had taken in many old and destitute women in its time, became the first sunset home in 1934. Some of its eighteen inhabitants had lived there before this. But there were many more as poor and deserving as these. Therefore the Sunset Homes Department was formed in 1935 to provide more homes for elderly women. Red House at Bootle, for many years a women's lodging house, was converted into a home similar to that in Boniface Street. Then a beautiful little house at Bovey Tracey in Devonshire was opened for those who were not quite so poor. A visitor, writing in 1960, describes this sunset home, which still operates beside the church of St. John the Evangelist:

> Both were built in Victorian days by the same benefactor in identical grey, quarry stone; both touching people's hearts with the love of God. The women who have made their home at St. Mary's are happy, well and busy. One has just begun an elegant green suit she is knitting for herself. She is eighty-three. Another looks after the large conservatory, with its hundred or more plants and the giant geranium beside the sitting-room door. There is always shopping to be done, the chapel to be looked after, the library list to be thought about for when the van comes, and the odd trip into town by the bus which stops at the door.

For elderly gentlewomen, the Hannah Symonds Home was opened in Bournemouth in 1937, combining the spaciousness of a large family house with the comfort of a private hotel. Each of the fourteen guests had her own room, but they shared the large sitting and dining-rooms. Among those living there in 1958, one had been a missionary in Japan, another the wife of a schoolmaster, and a third an ex-matron from one of the Children's Society homes. The need existed for a similar home in London, and in 1939 the Clapham Park Home was opened, only to be bombed two years later, with several casualties.

Daily living for elderly people in London was particularly difficult in wartime, for there were the added complications of blackouts and ration books. Therefore temporary homes were opened for those who could not manage at their own, at Merrow near Guildford, at Tulse Hill, and at Bow.

After the war, in spite of the extension of the social services, sunset homes were still required. Many old people did not qualify for the full rate of pension, their savings had shrunk by more than half with the decline in the value of the pound, and it had become increasingly difficult for their relatives to care for them. The Church Army started more homes, and most of these still care for some of the many elderly women in the community.

Horsell Lodge at Woking was opened in 1946, and Harleston House at Lowestoft the next year. Then, in 1949, Leinster Lodge at Putney became a sunset home, having as its first guests several of the old ladies who had survived the bombing at the Clapham Park Home and had spent the war years in Dorset. The bedrooms of this large Victorian house were divided into cubicles, each with its own wash-basin, and the garden was beautifully restored by an elderly gentleman from a neighbouring anchorage home. Today, television stands in the corner of the living-room, and a lift has been installed. Linnaeus House, Hull, and Holly Bush Lodge, Southgate, are more recent additions to the sunset homes. Holly Bush Lodge, which at one time had been a girls' training home, was adapted to make a most comfortable old people's home. The home for motherless children in Tunbridge Wells was converted, in 1960, into a home for frail elderly ladies who found it difficult to look after themselves. Here more nursing care could be given than was usual.

A sunset home of a different type is Kingsbury at Woking, which had been the home of Wilson Carlile's three sisters until 1956, and his home for the last eighteen years of his life. It is a short-stay home for people in temporary need. As the sister-in-charge says:

> It is quite different from the work in the usual sunset home because we are always starting all over again to know the newly-arrived guests and how best to help them. Some old people came as the result of a crisis in their own home, like the illness of a relative who normally looked after them, making it essential that someone else should take over the responsibility for the time being. Others came to Kingsbury until a permanent place could be found for them in a Sunset Home. Some, who could still "do for themselves" but had grown weary, arrive for a rest that will send them back renewed in body and spirit.

Most of them stay for only a few weeks and return refreshed and rejuvenated to their own homes.

Church Army captains and sisters, like many other people, find things difficult as they grow older, and therefore, in 1928, old-age pensions were introduced for them when they reached the age of sixty-five. A disability fund was also started for those who had broken down in health before reaching pensionable age and for the widows and children of those who had died while in the service of the Church Army. In 1937 it was decided to devote some of the money collected for the sisters' silver jubilee to building cottage flats for retired sisters, and by the next year the foundation stone for twenty-four of these flats had been laid at Bushey Heath in Hertfordshire. When Marie Carlile's memorial fund was raised in 1952, some of these sisters needed more specialized care, and so part of the fund was used to purchase and endow a house in Park Hill Rise, Croydon, where the older and more infirm sisters could live, and many now spend their last years in these pleasant surroundings.

As far as possible, the sisters in charge of these homes for elderly people try to make their guests feel part of the local community. The most active residents attend the parish church, and the congregation often takes an interest in the home, helping with minor repairs, and providing comforts and small luxuries. Members of the Rotarians, Toc H and other organizations come to entertain and talk with the residents, and Christmas parties are usually great occasions. This link with the outside world does much to keep them young in spirit, and to prevent the feeling of being shut away and unwanted.

The sisters have some knowledge of first aid and home nursing and usually attend courses arranged by the National Old People's Welfare Committee for those in charge of homes. Though they cannot be expected to undertake skilled nursing, they invariably have a sick room with twin beds, so that when anyone is ill or dying the sister-in-charge can be constantly with her. Thus, few have to end their days in hospital, and all can count upon the support of the sister when in serious trouble.

While there are many people in need of the care which the sunset homes provide, there are many others who could carry on much longer on their own if they lived in more suitable dwellings and were in reach of help if needed. As people grow older they cannot manage stairs, their landlady gets tired of helping or wants the room for someone who can pay a higher rent. Relatives may die, or the family increase in size so that there is no longer room for grandparents. It was people like this that Church Army Housing had in mind when in 1945 it decided to acquire large family houses and convert them into flatlets. Each person was to have a separate room and adequate space for a real home, with independence and privacy. She was to have a latchkey to her own door and to the front door. But some communal facilities were to be provided, and could be shared if wanted, and there was to be a sympathetic and unobtrusive management.

Sir Winston Churchill was asked to allow his name to be

connected with the scheme, and although he himself was too busy to take an active part, he delegated this to his daughter Mary, whose association with the Church Army had begun during the second world war. Two Churchill Houses, in Bristol and on Parliament Hill, Hampstead, were acquired with a donation from Sir Winston's eightieth birthday gift from the nation, many of the houses were opened by Mrs. Soames, and both she and Lady Churchill have been constant visitors to these Churchill houses.

In some cases the houses have been given outright by the donors, while others have been provided for in legacies, but usually Church Army Housing has had to purchase and convert houses itself, for no State subsidy can be claimed. Half the capital has been raised from loans, and the rest from the donations of individuals and organizations such as the National Corporation for the Care of Old People.

In 1945 and 1946 twenty-five houses were purchased in London, Reading, Sheffield and Stockport for conversion, and since then several purchases have been made every year, so that by 1965 there were over sixty houses, which had been converted into flatlets for more than six hundred and fifty people. They are scattered throughout England, as far south as Exeter and Southampton, and as far north as Newcastle. Several are in the Midlands, but the majority are in the London area where the need is particularly great. A few special trusts are also held by the Church Army Housing and run by them as part of the Churchill scheme. These include cottage flats for couples or single people at Enfield, an almshouse for nine men and four women at Ampthill, Bedfordshire, and some new flatlets for the elderly at Stoke-on-Trent.

A recent visitor to one of these houses gives her impressions:

I sensed the quiet joy of security the other day when I paid a visit to one of the Churchill Houses at Bristol. I met some of the elderly folk who are proud housewives in the flatlets which look out over the gay, well-tended garden, entirely cared for in her spare time by the house mother. On the edge of the lawn stood the almond tree, planted by Mary Soames, Sir Winston Churchill's daughter, when she declared the house open. Between the buttresses of the mellow wall which edged the garden on one side, some of the flat dwellers had their own plots. One boasted a flourishing runner bean plant among the flowers; later the owner proudly told me she had already had three dishes of beans from it. The entrance to the house was flanked with great tubs of blazing petunias. Here each member had her own small cubicle to which parcels of provisions could be delivered, and where her order for milk was placed each day.

The flatlets themselves, each with its shut-away cooking unit, containing deep sink, cooker, hot water supply, and ventilated larder, were furnished as diversely as fourteen highly differing individuals could make them. Here across the mantelpiece hung the beautiful long-stemmed ruby glass pipe that someone's grandfather had blown long ago; behind a glass cabinet the last treasured pieces of a family tea-set glowed in the sunlight; loved books ranged a shelf; a family of cacti stood on a tray in gay pots. Diversely as they were furnished, each home had one thing in common—its houseproud neatness.

Here fourteen old ladies, each in dire need of such accommodation, had found a haven, and each as an independent tenant with a yale lock on her door, but without any feeling of loneliness. The neighbourly feeling of a friendly community life was evident everywhere, even in the laundry room with its abundant hot water and spin dryer, which was a recent gift to the house. It was also in the flower-filled garden where the members could chat, and read, and knit, as they looked across the lovely grounds of Clifton College. And it was certainly in the house mother's own room to which the tenants are always welcome to come with their problems or to watch television, and where Christmas, the New Year, and birthdays always have their own happy celebrations.

Thus, the job of the house mother is to make the tenants

happy, and to be available if they are in any need. She shops for those who find it difficult to get out, accompanies any tenant who has to go to hospital, and visits her there, assuring her that her room awaits her when she returns. She is always ready for any difficulties in the flatlets, for tenants often lock themselves out, and minor accidents inevitably happen. Sometimes in the provinces a local committee manages the house, and then she is responsible to them in the first instance. Otherwise she is directly responsible to Church Army headquarters, and periodic housemothers' conferences are held there so that they may meet one another and learn from each other's experiences.

Those who occupy these flatlets come from many social groups, and include nannies, nurses, teachers, dependents of the clergy, professional women, and sometimes married couples who fear separation in old age. But they are all people who have little means, who are homeless or living in loneliness or discomfort, and they are usually unhappy and anxious before they come. A welfare fund is maintained by the help of subscribers to meet the occasional need. A tenant may be taken ill, or require temporary assistance in cleaning her room. She may need a taxi fare to hospital or clinic for treatment, and even with the help of national assistance there is little margin for such things on an old-age pension. Some require curtains, blankets or floor covering when they come to the flatlet; some need a short-stay visit to a rest home, and others the fare to make it possible for them to accept a holiday invitation. Even a wireless licence may make too large a hole in a weekly pension.

The tenants are expected to do their own housework and cooking, though in a few houses a midday meal is cooked and the flatlets cleaned for the tenants. For those no longer able to care for themselves, a rest home was opened at Highbury in 1949 in memory of Sir Frank Elgood, whose experience and knowledge had backed the original project of Church Army housing, and who had devoted much of his time to the Churchill houses. Although it was intended primarily for those tenants who had become too infirm to look after themselves, others are admitted who are awaiting hospital treatment, or are temporarily needing a rest. There are little luxuries like breakfast in bed, but it is not possible to give constant nursing attention.

Churchill houses, sunset homes, aged men's homes and special provision in the welfare hostels does not end the care which the Church Army offers to the elderly. There are many ageing people still in their own homes who depend upon the parochial sisters or captains for their main contact with the outside world, and for help in obtaining the services provided by the local authority. A sister discovered recently some elderly ladies in Kensington who were forced to vacate their rooms during the daytime. She opened a club room for them, with armchairs, papers and periodicals, so that they could spend the day there in the warm and make tea for themselves, returning to their rooms at night.

There are also those who have been brought up in comfortable homes and in educated families, but in old age or through long illness find that they can no longer entirely support themselves. Their sheltered lives have given them little understanding of financial matters; they are unable to live on what they have, or to realize that they should claim national assistance; they are bewildered, and unable to readjust their lives without help. The Church Army, through its Distressed Gentlewomen's Department, can offer unobtrusive advice and help, with the result that such people are able to live out the twilight of their lives with some feeling of security and love.

This care for the elderly is becoming increasingly necessary as the numbers of dependent old people rise and the pressure on local authority homes increases. The existing statutory and voluntary services for old people are quite inadequate to deal with all their needs, and the Church Army work for the elderly helps to add to the existing

provision. The Church Army always co-operates with the
welfare and public health departments of the local authority and so is able to provide supplementary services. But,
above all, the Church Army makes these elderly people
feel wanted and cared for, and this is often a step towards
an improvement in their well-being.

HELPING THE DISABLED

Care for the disabled developed from the work of the
Church Army during the two world wars, when most of
the normal work was closed down and much of the
Church Army resources were directed to the needs of
servicemen and women. The few remaining Church Army
captains, who had not been called up, and the majority of
the sisters were left to carry on the work in this country.
They often found themselves helping those who had been
sent back to England on account of ill-health or war
wounds, as well as those who had suffered from the bombing and the widespread devastation which it caused.

When hostilities came to an end after the first world war,
the Church Army was helping many whose disablement
made it difficult for them to find work. Then, in 1920, a
timely gift in memory of a wartime chaplain, the Rev.
T. B. Hardy, made it possible to convert the labour depot
in Star Road, West Kensington, into a hostel for disabled
servicemen. The difficulty now was to find some remu-
nerative occupation for them. This was solved when the
captain in charge of the Church Army employment bureau
happened to see in a shop window in the City a small
machine for colouring tissue paper. He realized at once
that since it could be worked with one arm it would be
suitable for men who were disabled and could be used
for making rose petals in a variety of delicate shades, to
be substituted for confetti at weddings. The next problem
was to encourage people to do this. Princess Mary helped
to solve it by using rose petals at her wedding in 1922. As

a result rose petals became fashionable at society weddings and the demand has continued, giving occupation to many badly disabled men.

At first the rose petals were made in a room in the central labour home in the Marylebone Road. It was soon found possible to make them in muslin as well as in paper so that they could be used for flowers sold on flag days. The making of name plates in hand-beaten copper followed, and these three forms of work supplied employment for the disabled for several years. Larger workrooms were rented in Penzance Place, Holland Park, and a room at headquarters used for the display of these rose petals, metal works and flowers to the public. When the Star workshop was built at West Kensington, it was possible to centralize the work there, and to introduce some forms of simple carpentry, the making of toys and other small articles. The motorized travelling shop and cinema carried examples of this work so that people outside London were made familiar with it.

After the second world war it was impossible to obtain permission to extend the workshops at West Kensington, and so at the end of 1945 the present buildings were taken over in Acre Lane, Brixton. Not only was there room to employ some fifty disabled men, but there was a hostel attached where thirty of them could live, and it was possible to find lodgings there for the more mobile of them. More workrooms enabled new industries to be tackled, such as tailoring, mattress making, and upholstery. In one workshop Church Army uniforms were made, mostly by men trained in tailoring before the war. In another room mattresses were repaired, and in the carpenters' shop and painting-room furniture for sale to the public and for the Church Army homes was constructed. A third room was devoted to upholstery; the metal shop produced a variety of goods, among them trays, candlesticks and other ornaments; and the making of rose petals was continued by the severely disabled.

The work has not changed greatly over the years. Ministry of Labour grants are now received towards the costs, but otherwise the Church Army has to meet the expenses, and is expected to continue to employ the man when he is trained.

On any day of the week you can walk into the workshops and find men with some quite serious disablement upholstering chairs, mending couches for hospitals, making mattresses for Church Army hostels. All these and many other jobs requiring training in craftsmanship are undertaken in conjunction with the Ministry of Labour, who sponsor the trainees for the first twelve weeks. Most of the furniture used in Church Army men's hostels is made here, and a recent job involved renovating wardrobes for some of the women's Church Army hostels. One man I met was deaf and dumb, but he was working away happily in the carpentry shop, and was obviously quite expert at his job. When men are really past learning a craft they are employed in some special occupational workshop learning simple jobs such as assembly work, or filing coupons for advertising schemes.

Many of the men are those disabled during the wars, but the younger ones have usually received their disability through an accident or as the result of polio or some other crippling illness. Though several other voluntary societies are doing similar work in close collaboration with the statutory services and the Ministry of Labour, there is no lack in the numbers of those who seek admission to the Church Army workshops; in fact there is not enough room for many of those who apply.

The Church Army social work therefore takes a variety of forms and includes the care of those who are on the fringe of society as well as serving the ordinary citizen. It tries not to overlap with what others are doing, but to fill in apparent gaps, to help people who have special needs, and to be ready for any sudden emergency. This is why its nature has changed over the years and why so often the function of a particular home has altered, pieces of work have been closed, and others have been started.

Of course, the Church Army's paramount interest is in the people it is trying to help, and so it is concerned with the spiritual as well as with the material aspects of all that it does. Prayer, therefore, forms an important part in the life of every captain and sister and in the organization of the different types of work. Communal prayers take place every day at 1.45 p.m. in the chapel at headquarters, Church Army officers pray regularly for the people with whom they come into contact, and a prayer leaflet for the various aspects of the work is used by the friends of the Church Army. Religion is not thrust upon anyone, but every home has its small chapel, usually a room which has been put aside and furnished for the purpose. No one needs to enter it, but most do at some time or other, and many find there the peace and joy which help to provide them with the strength they need in order to face their difficulties.

CHAPTER V

The Call of Other Countries

CHURCH ARMY METHODS have often evoked interest, and have sometimes been copied by other countries, as for example the Church Cross Army in Denmark. From the very early days officers of the Church Army volunteered for service overseas. In fact there is mention in 1888 of a captain being sent by Edward Clifford to India. They would use the methods of the Church Army in the countries where they went to work, and this would lead others to do the same.

But it was the Pan-Anglican Congress of 1908 which made Church Army methods more widely known throughout the world. The work of the different departments was on display in the Albert Hall, where many of the congress meetings were held, and the delegates were addressed on several occasions by members of the central staff. At the end of the congress, a two-day conference was held at headquarters, at which some overseas bishops were present.

As a result, several Church Army officers were invited to undertake short-term missionary work in Canada, India and China, using Church Army methods, and this voluntary secondment of Church Army officers for such work overseas took place intermittently until well into the 1920's, most of them working either with the Church Missionary Society or the Society for the Propagation of the Gospel, and then returning to the Church Army.

By this time several countries had become familiar with Church Army methods, and in the nineteen-twenties and thirties the Church Army itself began to take definite steps to extend its work to other countries. The evangelization of the world was very much to the fore in Christian thinking, and in its post-war reorganization the Church Army was ready to play a part in this expansion. Church Army work in the United States, Canada and India dates from the late twenties, and Church Army evangelists were also to be found in Sierra Leone, Tanganyika, New Zealand and Jamaica.

THE UNITED STATES AND CANADA

In 1924 a member of the board of the Church Army in England took a business trip to the United States, and met Bishop Manning, the Episcopal Bishop of New York. They discussed the importance of a lay ministry like that of the Church Army, and, as so often happened when the methods of the Church Army were described to overseas bishops, it was his first introduction to organized evangelism on a large scale by lay people. Other bishops heard about it, and eventually the Bishops of New York and Rhode Island asked whether some evangelists could be sent to America to demonstrate their methods. Twenty-four Church Army officers were chosen, under the leadership of Captain Mountford who carried on the work in the United States for many years, and Captain Casey who eventually went to Canada to start the Church Army there.

The leaders went ahead to plan the tour, which was to visit such places as Peekskill in New York state, New Haven and Hartford in Connecticut, Providence and several textile centres in Rhode Island, Concord in New Hampshire, Boston in Massachusetts and Portland and Waterville in Maine. When the evangelists arrived, they received a hearty send off from New York Cathedral. Captain Mountford writes:

This was our first public act of witness. With flags flying— Union Jack and Stars and Stripes—with our attention-

compelling red shields, indicating the points to which we
were pilgrims, with juvenile Captain Hanson and radiant
Arthur Casey leading, and with our really excellent five-
piece silver band pouring out martial music in a most
creditable manner, we marched through the City. Thus did
Broadway learn of our arrival.

After visiting places in New York City, the evangelists
divided into two columns at Peekskill, one going north to
Montreal and eventually sailing from there to England.
The other did a circular march through New England,
and returned to New York.

The next year a smaller group of evangelists was invited,
this time to visit the area around Washington D.C. After a
short time in Washington itself, they moved to Baltimore, then into Pennsylvania, and finally up to Montreal
from which port they returned to England in the late
summer.

All this prepared the ground for a visit of far greater importance. In 1926 Wilson Carlile himself came to the
United States and Canada. His visit greatly helped the
prestige of the evangelists, for as an ordained minister he
could plead their cause in the cathedrals and well-known
churches, and with his forceful personality he was able to
reach many who had no use for lay preaching. In fact, at
St. Thomas's, Fifth Avenue, he invited Captain Mountford to stand with him in the pulpit so that the congregation should realize that he regarded a lay preacher on an
equality with himself. In Washington he visited the President, and was invited to conduct the prayers at the opening session of the Senate, and in Baltimore and in Philadelphia he went to some of the poorer areas to see what
was being done for the people there. At Philadelphia, as
Captain Mountford so delightfully describes:

I thought I had the Chief safely tucked in bed, but after I
had retired, that holy rascal slipped out of the house late at
night, and trudged until he found the Galilee Mission and
saw something of the work undertaken there for the needy.

Having visited the United States, Wilson Carlile set off for Canada by way of Niagara, and on to Toronto and Ottawa, covering some of the ground which had been followed by Captain Casey and his eleven evangelists the year before. In Hamilton he preached on "Evangelism and Service", in Toronto he received the honorary degree of doctor of divinity, and in Ottawa he discussed Church Army plans for Canada with the Governor-General, after which he returned to Montreal en route to Britain.

Perhaps the words of the Bishop of Montreal at a dinner on the last day of his visit best describe the feelings of those who had invited him: "You are bringing us as great a contribution as a Bishop Temple or a Bishop Gore. We need your message, and your great contribution."

This was demonstrated in the United States the next year, when the bishops of the American Episcopal Church planned the "Bishop's Crusade", a nationwide evangelistic mission, with a team consisting of a bishop, a priest and a layman in each diocese. Bishop Perry of Rhode Island asked for a small team of Church Army evangelists to help him, and six were sent, who were allowed to speak not only in the streets, factories and the open air, but also in the churches. This crusade led to a request from certain New England bishops and clergy for the Episcopal Church to have a Church Army of its own.

So it came about that in a small room in the Gramercy Park Hotel in New York City, on December 12, 1927, the Church Army in the United States came into being with Mr. Samuel Thorne as its first president and an executive board of five bishops and several influential laymen. Captain Mountford was lent in the first instance for a period of five years to help with its organization, though it was twelve years before he finally retired. In March, 1930, the Church Army became incorporated under the laws of the state of New York, and the first training college was opened in Bishop McVicar House, Providence, Rhode

Island. It remained there until the premises at 414 East 14th Street, New York were acquired.

In Canada the situation was somewhat different. The Church Army was already known through its emigration work both before and after the first world war. At Winnipeg, Manitoba, there was already a hostel, in the charge of a Church Army captain and his wife, which received the boys on arrival, found jobs for them with the farmers in the district, and kept in touch with them until they were grown up. And at Haselton in British Columbia a group of Red Indians had formed a little band on Church Army lines, built their own hall, and were conducting their own evangelistic services. Therefore Captain Casey and his team of eleven evangelists were readily accepted.

His first visit was confined to the diocese of New Brunswick in the east, but his second, with twelve captains and eight sisters, was made to the dioceses of Montreal, Ottawa, Ontario, Toronto, and Niagara. This was followed, in 1928, by the invitation of the Archbishop of Huron for a group of ten captains and six sisters to visit every parish in his diocese.

After these crusades, the Anglican bishops decided to start Church Army work within the Anglican Church in Canada. This was made financially possible by Mr. Cyrus Dolph, who, hearing a sermon by Captain Casey in St. John's Church, Kitchener, Ontario, offered 10,000 dollars to start the work. He purchased a house, 143 Howland Avenue, Toronto for use as a training college, and on February 2, 1930, the Church Army in Canada was inaugurated with a service in St. Albans Church, Toronto. Mr. Dolph was its first president, with a committee appointed by the Archbishop of Toronto, and Captain Casey as field secretary.

Of the first eight cadets, who were commissioned in 1930, some went to the parishes, and others to evangelistic work, especially to the highway camps, which housed men on their way up country. Church Army vans were sent to the dioceses of Toronto, Ontario, Ottawa and Huron to reach the people in these extensive areas, and in many instances they were the only contact that some of the isolated farms had with the Church. In Toronto itself a certain amount of social work was done for the unemployed and for discharged prisoners. Conferences were held from time to time with the Church Army in the United States, and when Captain Casey left in 1935, the Canadian Church Army had become established.

Conditions within Canada have given to the Church Army there certain distinctive characteristics. The enormous parishes and lack of clergy have made it necessary for officers to take far greater responsibility for parochial work than in England and the United States, and this has meant that many have sought ordination in order to be able to carry out their work more effectively. Sisters have only recently been trained because much of the work has been among men in out-of-the-way places in the northwest, and comparatively little social work has been attempted in the big cities. The number of men coming forward for training has been small but reasonably constant, and in 1961, for the first time, two Cree Indians were commissioned, making some forty men in the field.

In the United States, the Church Army has progressed along more usual lines. The new headquarters at Brooklyn was opened in 1962, and consists of the office buildings, the church of the Holy Trinity, the training college, and a hostel. Visitors from this country always remark upon the warmth and friendliness which they find there, and on the care given to the development of personality, which forms an important part of their training.

> Students, cadets and officers all treat headquarters as their home, and sooner or later they all turn up again to see what's doing on Brooklyn Heights.

Of the ninety or so officers, scattered in work throughout the United States some are in charge of small, isolated rural or mountain missions; others are at work in settlement houses, in parishes as secretaries or as directors of religious education; others are at work in institutions and homes for delinquent boys and girls; whilst some carry out evangelistic work among all kinds of migrant workers.

A recent appointment was that of a sister to work among the Sioux Indians in South Dakota. Many of them were living in towns for the first time, and finding adjustment to town life particularly hard. The result of her work has been the coming forward of several Indian men for training as Church Army evangelists to take back the message of Christianity to their different reservations. It is in this way that the work of the Church Army has always grown, and as an Indian evangelist writes:

> I have conducted three street meetings and processions with them, and souls were won to Christ through their witness in their own tongue.

AUSTRALIA AND NEW ZEALAND

Like the United States and Canada, Australia and New Zealand have autonomous societies which are only loosely linked with their parent body in London. The first Church Army contact with this part of the world was in 1926 when two evangelists arrived in the diocese of Waiapu, New Zealand, to work among groups of men engaged in railway construction or hydro-electric extension work. In these camps there might be as many as five to eight hundred men who usually stayed only a short time before moving on to the next stage of the construction. Such out-of-the-way places would have no doctor, nurse or clergyman, and few of the men would have had any contact with organized religion. Thus there was plenty of scope for the Church Army officers, both of a practical and spiritual nature. Organized Church Army work in this part of the world did not begin, however, until the 1930's when teams of men and women evangelists from Britain were sent to both Australia and New Zealand.

In 1931, six English officers and two sisters, under the leadership of Captain Cowland, landed in Australia to tour the Commonwealth and conduct evangelistic missions in every state. As in America, their methods became widely known and were appreciated by the Anglican Church, so that in 1934 it was decided to start a Church Army in Australia, with "Skipper" Cowland, as he was affectionately called, to guide its early stages.

Headquarters were based at Tyrell House in Newcastle, New South Wales, and for twenty-five years the Church Army in Australia was directed from there. Federal offices were then established in Sydney, and the headquarters moved there in 1962. A training college was essential if Australian men and women were to be prepared for work with the Church Army in Australia, and from the beginning a house in Newcastle was used for the purpose. More commodious premises were then purchased in Stockton, New South Wales, where students were trained until 1961, when the college was moved to Croydon, a suburb of Sydney.

On account of the large distances, the work of the Church Army in Australia was at first very similar to that in America, and the mission vans have played an important part in evangelism, some of them crossing desert country to bring their religious films to the small groups of settlers there. Missions have been held in many small parishes, and often the Church Army officer has been the only representative of the Anglican Church that the people have met for long periods.

Church Army officers have also directed their attention to the towns, and undertaken tasks very similar to those performed in Britain. They have helped in children's homes, boys' hostels and hostels for apprentices; and industrial evangelism was started when a senior captain obtained permission to visit the state dockyards in Newcastle and a large industrial plant on the outskirts of Sydney. Following a visit to one of the English sisters at the Royal Free Hospital, an Australian sister was able to start a specialized ministry in the hospitals of Sydney in 1962. Captains and sisters have also moved into some of the new housing estates and inner-city parishes in Sydney.

An important part of the work of the Church Army in Australia has been among the aborigines. Captains and sisters have worked at such places as the Edward River Mission on the Gulf of Carpentaria, the South West Native Mission in Western Australia, and the North Queensland Mission station at Yarrabah. This has led in several instances to young aborigines entering the training college and returning when commissioned to work among their own tribes.

In New Zealand, it was 1933 before any attempt was made to extend the work which had begun among the construction people in the Waiapu diocese, although in 1931 the New Zealand Archbishop had consulted with the Church Army Overseas Department about the formation of an autonomous society in his province. Captain Barnyard and eight other captains and two sisters were invited to go to the Dominion to hold missions in as many parishes as possible, so that the people might become acquainted with Church Army work. Almost every parish was visited, with the result that the General Synod of 1934 passed a resolution "respectfully requesting the Bishops to do all in their power to forward such plans as may lead to the establishment of the Church Army in New Zealand".

The New Zealand branch became an autonomous society on November 4, 1935, with its headquarters in Auckland city. A training college was opened, and with the assistance of some English officers, New Zealanders were gradually trained and commissioned. Most of their pre-war work was evangelistic, and much of it carried on by the Church Army caravans which toured both the North and South Islands.

The second world war brought an end to this development, and it was some time before the Church Army was able to resume its activities. By 1953 the training college had been reopened and a number of Church Army officers were working in the parishes. A New Zealand captain paid a visit to Britain in that year to see something of the Church Army in this country, and after his return the Church Army in New Zealand gradually increased the scope of its work.

In 1959, the year of a visit of Edward Wilson Carlile, it was possible to reopen the Mission Caravan Department and to operate a caravan again in the diocese of Waiapu. Church Army officers had for some time taken a leading part in the running of the city missions in Christchurch and Auckland, and captains now become involved in evangelistic work in the prisons and military camps. But perhaps the greatest advance was in work among children, for, although boys' and girls' camps had been organized for some years, the arrival of a sister who had been in charge of the Children's Mission Department in England made it possible to extend this work and to introduce many new methods.

Comparatively little social work has been undertaken, although for some time the Church Army staffed the Henry Brett Memorial Home for Children at Takapuna, and during Edward Wilson Carlile's visit he opened a small home for old people in Hamilton. Work is done chiefly in connexion with the existing state social services, which have been well developed for a long time. One young captain writes:

> Perhaps the most rewarding of my services in His Name has been the social work; I have been made the local Anglican representative at all adult and children's courts, and this in turn leads to much work in conjunction with the police and child welfare department.

As in Australia, the present need is to extend the work among the aborigines, especially the Maori people. A sister writing about the huge Maori church festival—Hui Topi—in which she was invited to take part, describes "the free and easy hospitality they extend and the rigidly established rules for ceremonial welcomes, speeches and farewells". But there is also poverty, ignorance and hate, which can only be dispelled by having more Christian workers, particularly those from their own people. Money and manpower are needed, and although economies have been achieved in the last few years by sharing the Australian training college at Sydney, both money and manpower are still short.

INDIA

Work in India started at much the same time as in America. In February, 1927, two captains and two sisters, after a three month training at the Livingstone College in medical work, oriental phonetics and the religions of India, set sail for Madras to help the Indian Bishop of Dornakal who had visited England earlier that year. They were stationed at Khammamett while learning the language and, within six months, in true Church Army style and with the help of an interpreter, managed to preach to both Hindus and Christians. They had taken with them a gramophone and a few records in the language of the people around, and wrote home that "as soon as we got the gramophone on, people would come running from all directions, and in a few moments we had over fifty men and women, standing around, plus the never-failing innumerable children".

Once trained they had to concentrate upon medical work, which was the predominant need at that time, but one of the sisters helped to train the wives of ordination candidates so that they could work with their husbands in their future parishes.

In spite of the Bishop of Dornakal's desire to start a branch of the Church Army in India, he was never able to reach agreement with his fellow bishops, and all he could do was to train several men of his own diocese in Church Army methods. Sundaramma was the first native women worker to be trained. She had lost both her husband and her father in the same year, and in 1928 was sent to Dornakal for seven months to be taught by Mrs. Azariah, the bishop's wife. She then returned to work at her native village of Raghavapuram, where she was responsible for the care of women and children.

The Church Army was again involved in work in India in the late fifties when a sister was sent to help with the work at the Inter-Diocesan Moral Welfare home at Khammamett. The home provided a place of shelter and security not only for those who had moral difficulties, but also for those who needed care and protection, for in India the woman who has been turned out of her home is unprotected and unsafe even when in the care of an older woman. But Church Army work in India has never advanced beyond such isolated centres.

EAST AFRICA

The work of the Church Army on the African continent started in South Africa when in 1928 three officers were sent to the diamond diggings where some 20,000 white people and 200,000 natives were employed. Most of the families lived either in shacks made from petrol tins, mud canvas or corrugated iron, or in tents. Although a few fortunes were made, the majority of the people were very poor. Hence one of the officers reports:

> The Church Army, as friends of the poor, is faced with the enormous problem of relieving some of these conditions. Children, practically naked and half-starved, come to us for food and clothing. Children fainting and collapsing on the way to school are a common sight.

Much of their work was done in bars and saloons which had a thriving trade and, through the Sunday School

which they started they were able to get to know the
parents of the children. But when the diggings closed,
these Church Army officers were no longer needed there.

Tanzania was the next place to which the Church
Army went, for the first time in 1930. The Bishop of Tanganyika wrote in 1933: "I am writing this in the two-
roomed house of Captain Shaw, which is the beginning of
our new mission in Bugufi, 1,000 miles from the coast of
East Africa." Two years later a Church Army sister arrived
to start some medical work. The people among which she
worked were the Bahangazas,

> a strange tribe with a firm belief in witchcraft. Their way of
> dealing with sickness was to build little spirit houses, made
> with moulds of grass, to appease the spirits. These little
> houses they would build all around their own homes, and
> they fully believed that the little mounds would ward off the
> spirit which caused sickness of the body. The women had the
> most primitive way of dealing with childbirth, and with
> children, as the result of which many babies died. Still they
> looked on the white woman with suspicion, until at last she
> decided to win their confidence by placing a box on her
> verandah containing ointments, bandages and so on, and
> inviting them to come and see for themselves. Soon mothers
> were coming, bringing children for sores and burns to be
> dressed.

Slowly it was possible to establish a hospital and, more
important still, to train African maternity nurses who
could go out into the villages to help the women. This
work has continued, with its centre at the Kalinzi hospital,
where many midwives have been trained.

At Buigiri, near Dodoma, a school was started in the
early fifties for blind boys, most of whom need never have
been blind had it not been for malnutrition, the witch
doctor, and certain endemic diseases. Many came from a
local tribe, the Wagogo, but some from other tribes much
further afield. They all learnt to read braille in Swahili,
which is the lingua franca of East Africa, and many were

taught ordinary school subjects so that they could take the recognized examinations and eventually find work outside. Others, who were unemployable, remained at the school as "workers" and were engaged in making baskets, door mats, wool rugs, stools and other simple household utensils.

But much of the work of the Church Army in Tanzania was less spectacular, and consisted of continuous evangelism among the primitive tribes, often combined with medical help, for sleeping sickness and the more virulent forms of malaria were widely prevalent. A leper settlement was established where modern drugs were used, and the children protected so that they should not become contaminated. In this type of country medical missionary work is inseparable from evangelism, and through these methods many are won to the Christian faith.

Church Army work spread to Kenya in the winter of 1954–55. On account of the tribal disturbances, the government had gathered the people into locations, and conditions within these locations were very poor. Two sisters were, therefore, sent from Tanzania to Nairobi to see what they could do for the people in one of the locations. They wrote:

At first we were boarded out with a C.M.S. missionary on the Mission Compound, about four-and-half miles from our work, as the Government were very reluctant to allow us to rent an African house on the location, but a letter from the Chief Secretary of Kenya, explaining the position, soon procured the house for us. We would wish you could visit us and be shown over our little three-roomed bungalow. It is exactly the same as those used by the Africans around us. We are living in the midst of a people of various tribes and languages, e.g., the Wakikiyu, Waluo, Baganda, Wa-luia, Waembu, Wameru, and the Waswahili from Tanganyika, all living in our particular location. This is one of many, and all the menfolk are employed in one way or another in Government service. . . . We try to make our home a place where the African feels free to come in and see us at any time—not always about spiritual matters—maybe to beg an onion or a few matches.

In December, 1955, one of the sisters, while cycling across a level-crossing near their home during a fierce storm, was killed by a train. But this did not prevent the plans from going forward for a Church Army community centre in one of the poorest parts of Nairobi. A site was acquired in the suburb of Doonholm, near where the sisters had first settled, and on it was built a good-sized hall with kitchens adjoining, several class rooms, a chapel, a library, offices and a bookroom, as well as a small training college and a flat for the staff. The community centre was intended to be a place where the people of the neighbourhood could come together, and where their special needs could be met. Lack of employment is the scourge of this part of Africa, and it leads to much poverty and vice. Therefore, a variety of forms of work have been carried on, including literacy classes, teaching the boys and girls who have been unable to obtain a place in the school, feeding the hungry mothers and their children, providing sewing for those who can earn a living in this way, and training young people in commercial subjects so that they are more qualified for finding work.

With the present political and social progress, there is also a need to help the young married woman with the care of her children and her home. Classes in domestic science are given in the community centre, and since 1960 a sister has been engaged in organizing the work of the Mothers' Union in the diocese, since this is a most successful way of reaching the mothers, especially in the villages where Christian services are held.

Similar work was planned for Uganda with the building of a community centre at Katwe, on the outskirts of Kampala in 1964. People from all parts of East Africa, the Congo, Rwanda and Burundi are gathered here, many of them unemployed and living in the poorest of hovels. The centre was started by a group of Christians from the local

THE CALL OF OTHER COUNTRIES 161

churches, and gradually the buildings have arisen, including a large community hall, canteen, classrooms and workshops so that trades can be taught to the boys.

It has been realized for some time that Africans must be trained to take over all this work, and develop it along the lines needed in the future. It was for this purpose that the training college for these three East African countries was opened in Nairobi in the late fifties. At first only men were trained, but in 1962 two women entered the college, and in the same year the first two students came from Uganda. Now a number of men and women are in training, and the principal of the training college, who came to England for a year, is an African. It is probable that an African will soon become general secretary for the Church Army in Eastern Africa.

The work in East Africa covers a very wide area. The commissioned officers, over forty in number, are spread throughout the three countries of Kenya, Tanzania and Uganda, most of them in parochial work and some of them in very backward places. Several work in the prisons, as catechists in the Army, and on the mobile bookshop which sells African literature in the up-country towns and on the large farming estates. It is hoped that with the training of more sisters, a greater amount of case work can be undertaken with families in the rapidly growing urban areas, for here the broken homes are many, and drunkenness, prostitution and gross overcrowding produce many social and spiritual problems, very similar to those which the Church Army tackled in its early days in Britain.

THE CARIBBEAN

The Church Army had found its way to the West Indies some time before Edward Wilson Carlile visited the islands in 1954, but it was only as a result of his visit that it became organized in this area. Church Army methods had first been introduced to Barbados by a clergyman at

the beginning of the century, and when Edward Wilson
Carlile visited the island he found some twenty-five
branches with over 1,000 members, but, as his diary
showed, they only faintly resembled a Church Army elsewhere.

> They seem to meet for a weekly prayer meeting, visit the
> sick, and hold open-air services. The effectiveness of the
> evangelistic outreach depends on the Captain who is elected
> by the members annually. Some branches also appear to
> have a lieutenant. Some years ago there was no constitution
> and any Captain was quite free to take his battalion out of
> the Church if he so wished, but a previous bishop took the
> matter firmly in hand against a certain amount of opposi-
> tion, and there is an executive council consisting of all the
> Church Army chaplains—that is all the rectors who have
> a battalion in their parishes—and also three of the Captains.
> This council, of course, doesn't control the individual
> groups, but only the policy of the whole. It meets about
> once a quarter.

Describing a procession to the Cathedral he says:

> The women are all dressed in white, many of them with a
> broad-brimmed hat, with a red ribbon round it and the
> letters B.C.A. The Captains and lieutenants wear a sash, as
> a deacon wears his stole, and each of the twenty-five batta-
> lions has its own banner. A loudspeaker gives instructions
> and each battalion forms up in its allotted place, men in
> front and women behind. Four deep, they stretch right
> round the four sides of a large field and it is a most impres-
> sive sight. Then they set forth on the mile march to the
> Cathedral, with four men making the most appalling noises
> on some musical instruments. Towards the end there are
> several women enjoying themselves with tambourines.

In Trinidad, Edward Wilson Carlile found three indigenous Church Army officers who had been trained there
by an English officer several years before, and in Jamaica
there was an indigenous officer working among the
Indians. There was obviously some need for co-ordinating
the work in these different places, and for placing it on a

more stable basis. Bishop Gibson of the Kingston diocese in Jamaica had been aware of this for some time, and with some of his leading clergy and laymen he took the opportunity of discussing the matter with Edward Wilson Carlile. They suggested the possibility of West Indians joining the training course in England and then returning to their own countries to establish the Church Army there.

The outcome was that two West Indians came to the training college for two years training, and in the interval an officer was sent to help with the work in Trinidad and link it up with that in Barbados. The first Jamaican Church Army officer, Roy Wilson, sailed for Kingston in 1958 to lead a twenty-month diocesan mission, organized by the bishop, which would take him to all parts of the island. This has encouraged other West Indian men and women to come to England for training. It also led to the beginning of Church Army social work in Jamaica, for, as Captain Wilson writes:

> It seems that the immediate need for our workers in Jamaica is among the under-privileged peoples in the West end of Kingston. It is difficult to give a correct picture of this work, but it will be, in a real sense, slum work. Literally thousands of families living in small huts, crowded together, with very little material sustenance.

Hospital and prison visiting have now been organized, missions are conducted among the sugar cane workers in the cane fields, and a children's home has been staffed. When Prebendary Lynch visited Jamaica in 1964 the Church Army had become well established, and the bishop regarded it as his main evangelistic agency.

Thus, in all these territories, the Church Army has followed its usual pattern of seeking out the people in need and offering them both the Gospel and practical help.

Edward Wilson Carlile, like his grandfather, took a great interest in extending its work abroad, and during his ten years as chief secretary he was indefatigable in visiting all the countries concerned, in discerning their needs, and in suggesting ways in which the Church Army might help. It is largely due to him that the Church Army has become so well established in many countries overseas.

Today, missionary methods are changing, and the inhabitants of a country now want to be responsible themselves for taking the Christian message to their people. This is happening in the autonomous societies, where the original inhabitants are coming forward for training so that they may return as evangelists to their own people. It is also happening in territories like East Africa, where the control of the Church Army is gradually being handed over to nationals. This trend would have pleased Wilson Carlile, who believed in the evangelization of the people by the people.

CHAPTER VI

The Church Army Today

HER MAJESTY the Queen, when she opened the new headquarters in London on December 3, 1964, recalled the reasons for which the Church Army had been started in 1882, and for which it continues today:

> Its evangelistic and welfare work, which takes a wide variety of forms, supplements both the ministry of the parochial clergy and the welfare services provided by the State. To all these tasks its members come strengthened by their faith. In the field of social welfare, they are able to give practical expression to their Christian beliefs and bring comfort to people, many of whom may hitherto have been indifferent or unaware of the Christian message.

Today the Church Army is housed in an eight-storey block, ninety-three feet high, with a seventy-foot frontage on the Marylebone Road. Built on the site of the Yorkshire Stingo Brewery, it replaces the old labour home and welfare hostel which had been there since 1909. The plans for the widening of the Marylebone Road necessitated the demolition of the front of the hostel, and as the lease of the old headquarters in Bryanston Street was getting short, it was decided to find a more permanent site for the headquarters. Now this new building, in two tones of brickwork, with its bronze cross and flagstaff, dominates an area which, when the Harrow Road fly-over is completed, will be in a most central and strategic position.

Like so many other societies which had their origins in Victorian England, the Church Army has had to adapt itself to changing social conditions. It was born into a society which had wide differences, in wealth, in social class, in education and in behaviour. It has lived through two world wars, and now finds itself offering help to a community which is reasonably well off, where the State takes an increasing interest in the physical welfare of its citizens, and where the majority of the people see little sense in the Victorian presentation of religion. As the Very Rev. Martin Sullivan (now Dean of St. Paul's), said of the Church Army in 1963: "This is now a time of transition, new headquarters, new homes, new hostels and a more world-wide problem than ever before."

Such a situation would, no doubt, have delighted the heart of Wilson Carlile, who was always ready to adapt his methods to any circumstances, and yet was unflinching in his adherence to his basic principles. He would have been full of plans for reorganization, extension and improvement, which would have daunted the more prosaic members of the Church Army Board, but which would have met many of the needs of the rapidly changing structure of society.

Modern society is a materialistic society whose values tend to be linked to possessions. The increase in comfort and the rise in the standard of living have been phenomenal in the last few decades, which has meant that people are constantly striving to keep pace and are afraid all the time that their friends and neighbours will outstrip them. Clothes must be in the fashion, household equipment must be the latest, a car is indispensable and holidays abroad an essential. All these things need money to acquire and time to enjoy; and so life becomes an endless rush of earning and spending, with little time for rest and contemplation.

Perhaps for the first time in history religion no longer plays an important part in most people's lives. For one thing, many have only a vague understanding of its meaning and, unlike previous generations, have been taught little about it as children. Their only connexion with the Church may have been on some special occasion such as a wedding or a funeral, when it has been more a matter of custom than of personal belief. Furthermore, they seem to have managed quite well without religion, and so are not particularly interested in it. They may not have come into close contact with many churchgoing people who are so small a minority and, even if they have, they may not have found them particularly attractive. So it seems to them that Christianity has very little to commend itself.

Religion has always offered a sense of security in times of stress, and even this is shaken today when beliefs and moral standards are questioned. The "new theology" and the "new morality" introduce an element of uncertainty into the faith of even professedly Christian people, while others often feel engulfed by these moral and spiritual uncertainties. They are experiencing a state of inner turmoil, and yet may have a deep desire for something more definite by which to live. The young, in particular, feel this loss of direction and look restlessly around for some ideal to follow. Older people, bewildered by the pace of modern life and the speed at which it changes, frequently find the need for something beyond themselves and do not know where or to whom to turn for it.

Most of these people do not get the help they need from organized religion as it exists today, not only because they reject authority and religious sanctions, but because the words in which the Church speaks often mean little to the ordinary person. The Church's methods of communication are not those to which they are accustomed, and the Church does not seem to present its standards in a manner which has any close connexion with modern ways of living. Consequently, few of the people who most need a faith to live by bother to go near a church.

This situation is reminiscent of the early days of the Church Army when Wilson Carlile found that the Church meant nothing to most of the working people. Today, however, it is an even broader section of society which the Church fails to reach. Therefore the work which the Church Army has always been qualified to perform is still waiting to be done on the same lines as in the past and on an even greater scale. "Conversion, consecration, and churchmanship" are as central to the message as they used to be, but they have to be expressed in a new way and with a contemporary approach. Perhaps the most important thing of all is to keep the sense of urgency and whole-heartedness so characteristic of both Wilson and Marie Carlile, which they were able to pass on so effectively to those who worked with them. To them the Gospel message was as real and active as it was to the early apostles, and their success was undoubtedly due to their ability to demonstrate this living experience to all whom they met.

Wilson Carlile's method, to send the people to help the people, is also closely related to the modern trend which encourages the laity to take a more prominent part in the work of the Church and to undertake many things regarded in the past as the prerogative of the clergy. For years the Church Army has been training the laity in ways of reaching and helping people to know and understand the Christian message. It does so through its evangelistic week-ends and through the contemporary methods of approach which are characteristic of the programmes of Christian Advance. People from all Christian churches and all walks of life take part in these groups, and find themselves better equipped in every way to help those among whom they live and work.

Modern psychology teaches the importance and use of group methods, especially of the smaller groups where the members can become more fully acquainted with one another and, through their more intimate relationships, can more easily discuss their common problems. The Church Army is beginning to make use of these methods and to encourage the small group meeting in someone's house where the people can come to make friends and to discuss together the purpose of religion in their lives. Though there is still room for the larger evangelistic meeting, which often attracts a person in the first instance, these are being supplemented increasingly by the smaller, more intimate group.

Similarly, group ministries, where several churches in an area pool their resources, are also becoming more common, especially in the densely populated parts of the larger cities. When the Church Army officer is included in such a group, he will take on the special duties which would normally fall to an evangelist, and, being more free from the general responsibilities of helping to run a parish, he will have more time to get to know people and to reach those who have little interest in religion. Church Army officers, because of the special nature of their training and vocation, are particularly well equipped for such work, but if full benefit is to be gained from their ministry, they need to remain long enough in a given place to deepen friendships and to carry out their programmes to the full. Too often, the Church Army officer is invited to pioneer a particular piece of work, and then finds that once it is started his services are no longer required.

Church Army officers are increasingly called upon to undertake evangelism with special groups. Sisters have been invited to work with families on some of the new housing estates, and captains are beginning to do family welfare work. With the rapid growth in the numbers of immigrants, their care has become a new form of Church Army work, and since 1956 officers have met the boat trains which bring West Indians to London, and have helped them to make friends in the communities where they have settled. Captains have for some time worked as chaplain's assistants in the prisons, and sisters are now being asked to do similar work in the hospitals. For the first time, in 1959, a sister was appointed full-time, to work with patients in the Royal Free Hospital, and since 1966 another sister has been chaplain's assistant to a group of hospitals in Nottingham.

Similar work is being done in the armed forces. Though Church Army contact with the barracks at Caterham has a long history, a new step forward took place in 1961 when a Church Army captain was invited, under the auspices of the Royal Naval Lay Readers' Society, to work with the sailors at Portsmouth. This has led to similar appointments at Malta and elsewhere where many young naval personnel are stationed. The Church Army lay reader, since he has both training and experience, is able to relieve the chaplain of many of his heavier duties. Sisters are also taking part in such work, for in 1961 a sister was appointed, through the War Office, to Cyprus, where she helped with the spiritual, social and recreational activities of the Women's Royal Army Corps. It is quite likely that, in the future, more of these appointments will be made.

Rapid changes are also taking place in the social work field, for with the State assuming an increasing responsibility for the welfare of its citizens, voluntary societies have to fit in where they are still needed. The Church Army has always tried to care for people who would otherwise not be helped, and therefore throughout its history its forms of social work have altered with the changes in the work of the State and in that of other voluntary societies. Today it continues to adapt itself to those whose needs are not covered fully by the existing social services, as in its care for prisoners' families and the provision of holiday homes.

In our affluent society, far fewer people are in material want, though, as in the past, such needs are always heeded by the officers and sisters, and met in so far as this is possible. Today, personal problems rather than material want trouble most people. People move frequently from place to place, young people like to live away from home, and older people can less easily stay with relatives. So human relationships tend to become superficial and friendships shallow, and many feel isolated and lonely. When they are in trouble or difficulty they often do not know to whom to turn. Through its different forms of work and its many contacts, the Church Army is able to discover many of these people and to offer them such help and understanding as will enable them to cope with their particular situation.

Others may be driven to anxiety and despair, or to excess drinking and the taking of drugs; and the authorities can do little for such people. Since its beginnings, the Church Army has helped people in dire distress. "Go for the worst" was a favourite saying of Wilson Carlile, and this has always been the policy of the Church Army, though it might not be expressed in exactly these terms today. The modern method of dealing with such problems, which are often spiritual and emotional, is counselling. Number 5 Cosway Street, opposite the new headquarters, has been opened as a counselling centre for all who need this type of help, and the work of Bethany has been transferred to the same premises so that many of the women who battle against drink and drugs can benefit from it. Similar methods are used in the centre for crude spirit drinkers which has now been opened in another part of London.

Another important need today is the provision of homes for people who, for different reasons, cannot continue living in their own homes. They may be too old, they may have just come out of prison or hospital and have nowhere to go, or they may be the sort who cannot settle down to the ordinary routine of life. State provision for such people is meagre, and the State relies on voluntary societies to help. The Church Army is particularly suited for residential work, for in a society which is becoming increasingly impersonalized its training has a place for the art of homemaking and for an understanding of the ordinary things of life. Because the officers look upon their work as a Christian vocation they are available at all times of the day and night, if they are needed, and are willing to help with any kind of difficulty. Nothing is too much trouble, and they offer kindness and compassion wherever these are required. Thus they produce in their homes for old people, their welfare hostels, their special homes for young mothers, for professional people and for the disabled, an atmosphere of contentment and happiness which few fail to appreciate. This may be the special contribution which the Church Army has to make to the social services of the future, for it is unlikely that the authorities will be in a position to meet this need themselves for a very long time.

In spite of the different types of work which the Church Army offers, the number of suitable men and women applying for training is small and by no means sufficient to fill the posts open to them. With less than five hundred captains and sisters in the field, this is an urgent problem. There has always been a demand for more workers, but it is particularly the case now when many of the older workers who were recruited after the first world war are retiring and comparatively few are coming along to fill their places.

In the past, the Church Army was often the only form of full-time Christian service available for the man who did not possess the educational qualifications for ordination. Today, with greater improvements in education and less rigid requirements for ordination candidates, this is no longer the case. Similarly, there used to be a number of women without home duties, but with the proportions of men and women more equally balanced in the population, this is not so today. Arrangements have therefore been made whereby sisters who marry may, under certain conditions, retain their commissions and continue with their work. This is in line with modern ideas, and it is often a very suitable arrangement when a married couple are in charge of a "home", or when the services of a sister are greatly needed in the community where she lives.

The new Church Army training college may help to attract the modern man and woman, for it occupies a two-acre site on the edge of Blackheath Common. Opened by Princess Alexandra early in 1965, it is a memorial to Wil-

son Carlile and called by his name. Architecturally, the
College is a blend of the old and the new, being a large
Victorian house with a new residential wing of attractive
and commodious study-bedrooms for more than seventy
students. Its chapel, with a beautiful roof in the shape of a
shell, is built in modern style with long slit windows of
deep gold and a blue cross-shaped window above the
Communion table. Its grounds and tennis courts make its
surroundings pleasant for those who are returning to study
for a period.

The training is being adapted to suit modern needs and
to bring it more closely into line with that provided by
other bodies for similar types of work. The period has been
lengthened to three years, and this should make it easier to
cover fully both the theological and the social aspects and
also to provide concentrated periods of practical experience
in all the fields of Church Army work. The training before
commissioning is intended to be basic and, from the theological aspect, to equip the student as evangelists as well as
helping them to meet the special pastoral needs which they
will encounter. The social side should give the student a
working knowledge of the social services and other forms of
social work, with some understanding of the growth and
development of the human personality. Those needing
special skills are already attending courses at Josephine
Butler College, and the youth leaders' training at the
National College at Leicester, and it is hoped that these,
with perhaps some more precise training in residential
social work, will form part of the post-commissioning
training for those engaged in these special forms of social
work. The possibility of short courses of refresher training
is to be welcomed, for, in these days of rapid change, it is
essential to keep up to date.

The Church Army has the difficult task of providing
two separate and different types of qualification. As the
training for professional social work becomes more uni-
versally required, its teaching standards will need to reach

those of the professional bodies, and more officers will have
to take advantage of the outside courses and qualifications
which are available. At the same time its primary duty is
evangelism, and this can never be neglected if it is to remain true to the memory of Wilson Carlile. It is not intended to produce prodigies of learning, for Church Army
students are selected for their sense of vocation and committal to the Christian faith, rather than for their aca-
demic knowledge. But its future officers must be able
to take their place in a world which requires increasing
attention to adequate training.

Church Army captains and sisters have the great privilege of playing a unique part in the life of modern society,
both in England and in those other countries where the
Church Army has been invited to serve. For their concern
is not with policies or with institutions, but with individual
people. They believe that if a person is to achieve his full
potential in life and is to be really helped in his difficulties,
whatever these may be, he needs a living faith in a personal God. Only thus can he become a complete person;
and this is so, whether he is weighed down by the difficulties of life, is handicapped in some way, for some reason
does not fit into the conventions of society, or is just an
ordinary person who feels that there is something lacking
in his life. This is the belief of all captains and sisters, who
always stand ready to help others, not only as a social
duty, but in order to show them something of the love of
God.

BIBLIOGRAPHY

D. H. BARBER, *The Church Army in World War II*, S.P.C.K., 1946.

MARY BURN, *The Pearl Divers*, Marshall Bros., 1920.

E. WILSON CARLILE, *From Canada to the Caribbean*, 1955.
East African Safari, 1958.

WILSON CARLILE, *Boanerges and Others*, 1932.
The Early Days of the Church Army 1883–1886, 1891.

R. CHOLMELEY, *Edward Clifford*, 1907.
The Church Army in Action, published for the Lambeth Conference, 1958.
The Church Army on Active Service, 1946.

EDWARD CLIFFORD, *A Blue Distance, or Letters to Comrades*, 1899.
A Green Pasture, Second series of Letters to Comrades, 1901.
The Wounded Heel, 1906.

SIDNEY DARK, *Wilson Carlile, the Laughing Cavalier of Christ*, Clarke, 1944.

KATHLEEN DAVIS, *Holloway Prison was my Destiny*, 1949.

J. K. V. DURRELL, *Whizz Bangs and Woodbines*, Hodder and Stoughton, 1918.

HALE and CAVE. *Yours is the Fight*, 1945.

E. HANMORE, *The Curse of the Embankment.* P. S. King, 1935.
Out of the Depths, 1939.
A Mobile Army of Evangelists—The Church Army in Australia, 1963.

A. E. REFFOLD, *The Audacity to Live*, 1938.
Great Churchmen—Wilson Carlile, 1947.
A Noble Army of Women, 1947.

A. E. REFFOLD, *Seven Stars*, 1931.

    Wilson Carlile and the Church Army, 5th edition, 1956.

    Roof Overhead—Twenty-five years of Church Army Housing, 1950.

W. SPENCER, *The Other Side of the Prison Gate*, Marshall, Morgan & Scott, 1938.

PHYLLIS THOMPSON, *Within a Yard of Hell*, 1964.

LETTICE THOMSON, *Mary Burn, An Appreciation*, 1936.

    A Thread of Gold, 1936

    Work Aid, 1920.

Where no publisher is stated, the books are published by the Church Army Press.

PERIODICALS

Church Army Annual Reports 1885–

Church Army Gazette (with its predecessor *The Battleaxe*), 1886–1962.

Church Army Review (with its predecessor *Church Army Quarterly Paper*), 1894–

Our Quarterly (with its predecessor *Letters to Church Army Officers*), 1905–

Spearhead, 1955–

The Anglican Crusader, The Church Army in Canada.

The Pioneer, The Church Army in Australia.

Workers Together, The Church Army in New Zealand.

Index

Albion Hill Homes, Brighton, 85
Alexandra Club, 102–3
Anchorage Homes, 133
Approved schools for girls, 120–1
Australia, 152–4, 155

Banner and Art Department, 54
Barmaids' Rest, 104
Barnyard, Captain, 154
Barrow, Mrs. Sowton, 123, 125
Belvedere House, 80, 118
Bethany, 48, 91, 171
Better Britain Brigades, 107–8
Bodelschwingh, Pastor von, 59
Bookroom, 55–6
Booth, Charles, 15, 57
Booth, General William, 60
Bovey Tracey Home, 134
Boys' Aid, 65, 107
Brookfield House, 106
Brunswick Chapel, 27
Bryanston House, Nottingham, 121
Burn, Mary, 53, 107

Canada, 148, 150–1
Canteens, 68, 79, 104, 132
Carlile, Edward Wilson, 37, 155, 161–3
Carlile Lodge, Folkestone, 101

Carlile, Mary, 23, 136, 168
Carlile, Mrs. Wilson, 22
Carlile, Wilson, 11–25, 36, 38, 47, 49, 53, 57, 60, 76, 123, 125, 148, 164, 166, 167, 168, 171, 174
Caribbean, 28, 161–4, 169
Carr-Glyn, Dr., 14, 16
Caterham Barracks, 170
Casey, Captain, 147, 150–1
Cheshire, Mary, 23, 54
Children's Missions, 44–7
Christian Advance, 50–1, 168
Church "Army", 17–18, 165–174
Church Army captains, 32, 90, 170
Church Army Gazette, 52–3, 84, 107
Church Army headquarters, 21–2, 64, 165
Church Army Housing, 122–31, 138
Church Army officers, 17, 28, 46, 69, 100, 121, 122, 136, 141, 146, 169, 172
Church Army sisters, 27, 32, 40, 45, 71, 90, 114, 116, 118, 169, 172
Church Army Review, 8
Church Army Scouts and Guides, 108
Church Army social work, 20, 57–145, 170
Church Army training, 26, 28–30, 109, 172–4

Church Army Training College, 27, 28, 172–3
Church Congress, 18–19
Churchill Homes, 137–142
Churchill, Sir Winston, 138–9
Church of England Advisory Board for Moral Welfare, 86–7
Church Parochial Mission Society, 17, 21, 23
Church Penitentiary Association, 85
City gardens, 64–5
Clergy homes, 100
Clifford, Edward, 23, 146
Clifton House, 72
Clothing Department, 92–3
Clubs for girls, 102–6
Counselling centre, 92, 171
Court Moor Home, Fleet, 97, 133
Crathorne House, Finchley, 88
Crossed Swords Club, 110–11
Cowland, Captain, 153

Davey, Captain, 113
Daylight cinema, 37, 55, 143
Disabled, 142–5
Discharged Prisoners' Aid societies, 117
Distressed Gentlewomen's Department, 82, 141

East Africa, 28, 157–161
East London Home, 80
Elgood, Sir Frank, 124, 126, 140
Elgood House, 80
Embroidery Room, 54
Emergency hostels, 80–1
Emigration, 60, 65–6
Evangelization Society, 14
Evangelistic missions, 35–8

Evangelistic week-ends, 47–9

Fleetwood Youth Centre, 110
Flying Columns, 37–8
Frances Owen Home, 88
Fresh Air Fund, 95

Gay, Evelyn, 23, 90
Gipsies, 41, 84
Godstone Home, 96, 102
Gordon Boys' Home, 102
Group ministries, 169

Hannah Symonds Home, Bournemouth, 134
Hardy, Rev. T. B., 142
Hempstead Hall, 62, 65, 120
Holiday homes, 96–9
Holly Bush Lodge, Southgate, 89, 135
Hopkins, Rev. Evans, 16
Horsell Lodge, Woking, 135
Hospital visiting, 44, 163
Hostels for girls, 106
Housing estates, 32–4, 169

India, 156–7

Josephine Butler College, 86

Kennedy, Rev. J. Studdert, 125
King George's Embankment Home, 68–9, 74
King's labour tents, 63–4
Kingsbury, Woking, 23, 136

Labour homes, 57, 62, 63, 67, 69, 112, 142
Lads' hostels, 119
Lantern Department, 54
Leinster Lodge, Putney, 135
Linnaeus House, Hull, 135

Livingstone House, Stone-bridge Park, 73, 93
Lodging houses, 61, 75, 132, 143
London College of Divinity, 14

Mackirdy House, 106
Matthews, Dr. W. R., 24–5
Medical Mission, 94–5, 96, 102
Moody, D. L., 13, 14, 23
Moral welfare, 48, 84–7, 90
Motherless children, 101–2, 135
Mothers' Union, 33, 41, 54, 160
Mountford, Captain, 147, 148

Nelson Square Centre, 74, 106
Newdigate Farm, 62
News teams, 49–50
New towns, 35
New Zealand, 152, 154–6
Night shelters, 62–4, 69–70, 74

Open-All-Night Shelter, 64

Parkside, Huyton, 120–1
Parochial work, 30–5, 168–9
Pensioners' rooms, 132
Peter House, Westminster, 78–9
Portman House, 80, 91
Princess Club, 104–5
Printing press, 53–4
Prior, Captain, 38
Prisoners' families, 115–17
Prisoners on release, 76, 117–18
Prison chaplains' assistants, 114–15
Prison missions, 113

Prison visiting, 113, 114, 163
Probation, 75, 118–20
Professional men's hostel, 76

Queen Elizabeth Lodge, Southgate, 120
Queen Lodge, 80
Queen Mary Hostel, 79–80
Queen's relief depots, 64

Red House, Bootle, 118, 134
Reformatory and Refuge Union, 85
Rescue homes, 84–5
Rose Restaurant, 106
Royal Free Hospital, 169
Royal Naval Lay Readers' Society, 170
Ruggles-Brise, Sir E. J., 112

St Ann's Home, Wandsworth, 87, 88
St. Helena's, Margate, 85
St. Mary Abbots, Kensington, 14, 16, 26, 57
St. Mary-at-Hill, 22, 47, 106
St. Monica's, Croydon, 87
Salvation Army, 17, 60
Sanatorium, 95, 129
Seasalter Camp, 99, 108
Soames, Mary, 138, 139
Social Centres, 66–7
Social security, 74, 93, 132, 144, 170
Spearhead, 53
Spencer, Captain, 113
Stafford County Home, 120
Stanley House, Stonebridge Park, 65, 83, 120, 125
Star Road, West Kensington, 69, 142
Sullivan, Very Rev. Martin, 166
Summer crusades, 42–5

Sunbeam Mission, 93–4, 102
Sunnyland Club, 105
Sunset Homes, 134–7, 141, 172
Sunshine, Hurstpierpoint, 101

Temperance homes, 90–1
Training homes for girls, 89
Tramps and Inebriates Home, 60
Treacher, Prebendary, 24, 76
Trewint, Bexley Heath, 89
Turner House, 87, 106

United States, 147–8, 149, 151

Vans, 38–41
Visual aids, 55

Walmer House, Notting Hill, 65
Walworth Mission, 18

Waterloo Road Shelter, 69–70
Wayside lodges, 72
Welfare hostels, 75–6
Westminster Mission, 18
White Hart, 81
Wilson Carlile House, Stepney, 71–2, 73
Wilson, Captain Roy, 163
Women's Embankment Home, 80, 134
Women's Help Department, 77
Women's hostels, 78–81
Women's Royal Army Corps, 170
Work-aid Homes; see Labour Homes
Workhouses, 59, 87, 112, 124, 132

Yorkshire Stingo Brewery, 22, 64, 165
Youth centres, 109–11